ORGAN HISTORICAL SOCIETY
EMPIRE STATE
HYMNBOOK

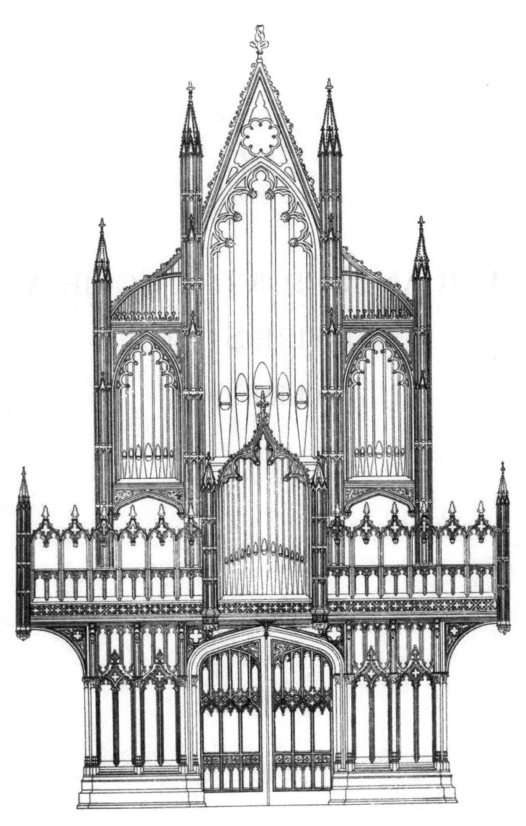

The Richard Upjohn case of the 1846 Henry Erben organ of Trinity Church
drawn in 1896 by Edward Necarsulmer (1874–1959)

Organ Historical Society

Empire State

Hymnbook

Compiled, Edited, and Annotated

by

Rollin Smith

COVER PHOTOGRAPHS BY LEN LEVASSEUR
Front: The Craighead-Saunders Organ
Back: The 1893 Hook & Hastings Op. 1573
Christ Church, Rochester, New York

Organ Historical Society
330 North Spring Mill Road
Villanova, Pennsylvania   19085-1731
organhistoricalsociety.org
804-353-9226

Copies of this book may be obtained from
www.organhistoricalsociety.org

CONTENTS

CONTENTS

ILLUSTRATIONS

THE CHURCH TRIUMPHANT, AND THE CHURCH BELOW,
IN SONGS OF PRAISE THEIR PRESENT UNION SHOW;
THEIR JOYS ARE FULL, OUR EXPECTATIONS LONG,
IN LIFE WE DIFFER, BUT WE JOIN IN SONG;
ANGELS AND WE, ASSISTED BY THIS ART,
MAY SING TOGETHER, THOUGH WE DWELL APART.

Edmund Waller, *Of Divine Poesy*

PREFACE

Just compiling a list of composers active in New York City and State is a daunting task and likely one never to be completed successfully. Then add a list of organists and those who composed hymn tunes and the number is astounding. The present compilation is modest compared with the resources available, but is limited to music in the public domain.

We thank composers who graciously submitted hymns for inclusion in this book: Agnes Armstrong, Stephen Best, Matthew Bellocchio, Frederick Grimes, the late McNeil Robinson, and F. Anthony Thurman; and we are particularly grateful to those who have composed hymns especially for this hymnbook: Anthony Baglivi, Carson Cooman, Alfred V. Fedak, Sebastian M. Glück, David Hurd, Hampson Sisler, Frederick Swann, and Julian Wachner.

Of particular interest in this collection, are hymns that mention the organ in the text. Organbuilders Matthew Bellocchio and Sebastian Glück wrote their own texts, giving the organ prominence; Alfred Fedak wrote on a text by Timothy Dwight; while David Hurd and Frederick Swann both utilized Godfrey Thring's 1874 poem *An Organ Hymn.*

The collection is not limited to organists, but includes hymns by noted composers, conductors, singers, pianists, literary figures, and several men involved with the Aeolian Company, all of whom were also organists.

Modern hymnals abound with hymns by contemporary New York musicians, but we hope with this hymnbook to have brought to light some worthy examples by famous organists of the past two hundred years as well as to have contributed some outstanding newly-composed additions to this ever-growing repertoire.

The editor would like to acknowledge the valuable assistance of Todd Sisley, editor the *The American Organist,* in proofreading this book.

ORGAN HISTORICAL SOCIETY EMPIRE STATE HYMNBOOK

With One Accord Thy Praise We Sing

1

Official Song of the Aeolian Employees' Association

AN AEOLIANITE, 1916

SILESIAN FOLK SONG, 16th cent.
"O Tannenbaum"

1. With one ac - cord Thy praise we sing, Ae - o - li - an!
2. Since those old days down on Broad - way,* Thy fame has spread, Ae - o - li - an!
3. Our best we glad - ly give to Thee; Ae - o - li - an!

All hon - or to Thy name we bring, Ae - o - li - an!
Our Pres - i - dent† has led the way, Wise were his steps, Ae - o - li - an!
We owe Thee deep - est loy - al - ty, Ae - o - li - an!

Thy pol - i - cies good faith in - still, Thy in - stru - ments are works of skill
Now from Thy Hall's‡ im - pos - ing height, A word gleams forth in gold - en light —
No shad - ow mars Thy his - to - ry, Thy Stand - ard Bear ers let us be,

We pledge al - le - giance with good will —
A word which stands for truth and right; Ae - o - li - an! Ae - o - li - an!
Long live our no - ble Com - pa - ny —

* The first address of the Aeolian Company was 831 Broadway, between 12th and 13th streets.
† Harry B. Tremaine (1866–1932), son of the founder.
‡ The 17-story Aeolian Building was at 29–33 West 42nd Street in New York.

13

Gather Us In, Thou Love That Fillest All

WHITNEY 10 10. 10 10. 44

GEORGE MATHESON, 1842–1906

MARK ANDREWS, 1860–1932

With dignity

1. Gath - er us in, Thou Love that fill - est all, Gath - er our
2. Gath - er us in: we wor - ship on - ly Thee; In var - ied
3. Each sees one col - or of Thy rain - bow light, Each looks up -
4. Some seek the fath - er in the heav'n a - bove, Some as a

riv - al faiths with - in Thy fold, Rend each man's tem - ple's veil, and
names we stretch a com - mon hand; In di - verse forms a com - mon
on one tint and calls it heav'n; Thou are the full - ness of our
hu - man im - age to a - dore, Some crave a spir - it vast as

bid it fall, That we may know that Thou hast been of
soul we see; In ma - ny ships we seek one spi - rit -
par - tial sight; We are not per - fect till we find the
life and love; With - in Thy man - sions we have all and

In Unison   *In Harmony*

old;
land;   Gath - er us in,   Gath - er us in.   A - men.
sev - en;
more;

This Is the Day of Light

ARETTA S. M.

3

JOHN ELLERTON, 1826–1893

FREDERIC ARCHER, 1838–1901

1. This is the day of light: Let there be light to-day;
2. This is the day of rest. Our fail-ing strength re-new;
3. This is the day of peace: Thy peace our spir-its fill;
4. This is the first of days: Send forth Thy quick 'ning breath,

O Day-spring, rise up-on our night, And chase its gloom a-way.
On wea-ry brain and trou-bled breast Shed Thou Thy fresh-'ning dew.
Bid Thou the blasts of dis-cord cease, The waves of strife be still.
And wake dead souls to love and praise, O Van-quish-er of death!

When All Thy Mercies, O My God

4

AMHERST C. M.

JOSEPH ADDISON, 1672–1719

HOMER N. BARTLETT, 1846–1920

1. When all Thy mer-cies, O my God, My ris-ing soul sur-veys,
2. Oh, how shall words with e-qual warmth The gra-ti-tude de-clare,
3. Ten thou-sand thou-sand pre-cious gifts My dai-ly thanks em-ploy;
4. Through all e-ter-ni-ty, to Thee A joy-ful song I'll raise;

Trans-port-ed with the view, I'm lost In won-der, love, and praise.
That glows with-in my rav-ished heart? But Thou canst read it there.
Nor is the least a cheer-ful heart, That tastes those gifts with joy.
But oh, e-ter-ni-ty's too short To ut-ter all Thy praise!

5 Praise the Lord from the Heavens

ALTAMONT Irregular

PSALM 148
Paraphrased by AGNES ARMSTRONG

AGNES ARMSTRONG

1. Praise the Lord from the heav'ns, Praise the Lord in the heights, Praise the Lord, all His
2. Praise the Lord from the earth, Praise the Lord from the seas, Praise the Lord from the
3. Praise the Lord, hu-man-kind, Praise the Lord day and night, Praise Him, wom-en in

hosts, O praise Him, you an - gels bright. Praise the Lord, sun and moon, Praise the
hills, O praise Him, moun-tains and trees. Praise the Lord, fire and hail, Praise the
joy, O praise Him, men with de - light. Praise the Lord, crea-tures wild, Praise the

Lord, shin-ing stars, Praise the Lord now with high de - light, Let the name of the
Lord, snow and fog, Praise the Lord, storm - y wind so free. Let the name of the
Lord, man and child, Praise the Lord, young and old, u - nite. Let the name of the

Lord be ex - al - ted and praised, who cre - a - ted us all a - right.
Lord be ex - al - ted and praised, who com - mand-ed us by de - cree.
Lord be ex - al - ted and praised, who e - ter - nal-ly rules in might.

O Christ, Who Holds the Open Gate

QUI TENENT L. M.

JOHN MASEFIELD, 1878–1967

EDWARD SHIPPEN BARNES, 1887–1958

1. O Christ, who holds the o - pen gate, O Christ, who drives the fur - row straight, O Christ, the plough, O Christ, the laugh - ter Of ho - ly white birds fly - ing aft - er.

2. Lo, all my heart's field red and torn, And thou wilt bring the young green corn, The young green corn di - vine - ly spring - ing, The young green corn for - ev - er sing - ing.

3. And when the field is fresh and fair Thy bless - ed feet shall glit - ter there, And we will walk the weed - ed field, And tell the gold - en har - vest's yield,

4. The corn that makes the ho - ly bread By which the soul of man is fed, The ho - ly bread, the food un - priced, Thy ev - er - last - ing mer - cy, Christ.

7 God of the Morning

THE ETERNAL GOD L. M.

G. E. IRELAND

ANTHONY BAGLIVI, b. 1944

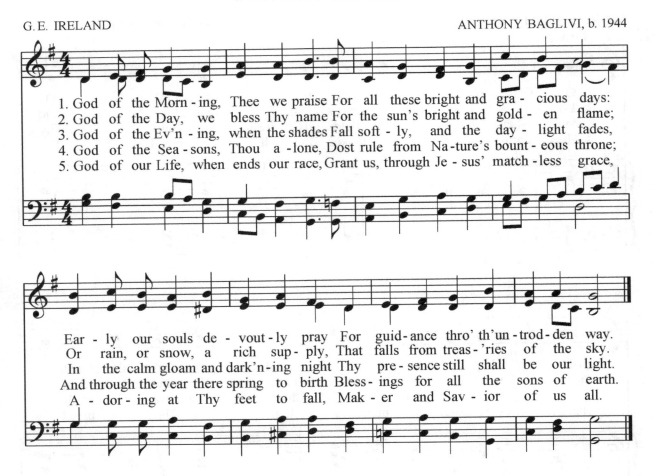

1. God of the Morn - ing, Thee we praise For all these bright and gra - cious days:
2. God of the Day, we bless Thy name For the sun's bright and gold - en flame;
3. God of the Ev'n - ing, when the shades Fall soft - ly, and the day - light fades,
4. God of the Sea - sons, Thou a - lone, Dost rule from Na - ture's bount - eous throne;
5. God of our Life, when ends our race, Grant us, through Je - sus' match - less grace,

Ear - ly our souls de - vout - ly pray For guid - ance thro' th'un - trod - den way.
Or rain, or snow, a rich sup - ply, That falls from treas - 'ries of the sky.
In the calm gloam and dark'n - ing night Thy pre - sence still shall be our light.
And through the year there spring to birth Bless - ings for all the sons of earth.
A - dor - ing at Thy feet to fall, Mak - er and Sav - ior of us all.

8 All Hail the Pow'r of Jesus' Name

86 86. 86 86

EDWARD PERRONET, 1726–1792

AMY BEACH, 1867–1944

Mæstoso alla Marcia ♩ = 84

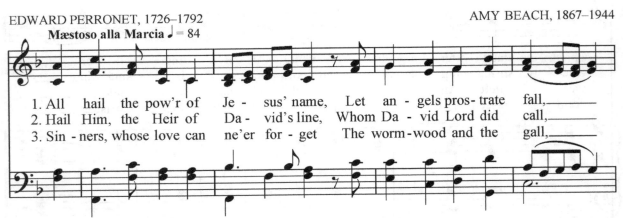

1. All hail the pow'r of Je - sus' name, Let an - gels pros - trate fall,_____
2. Hail Him, the Heir of Da - vid's line, Whom Da - vid Lord did call,_____
3. Sin - ners, whose love can ne'er for - get The worm - wood and the gall,_____

O God, We Thank You

CORAM HALL 86 86. 86 86

MATTHEW M. BELLOCCHIO, b. 1950

MATTHEW M. BELLOCCHIO, b. 1950
harm. GEOFFREY MORGAN

Tubas 8', 4' Great Tubas 8', 4'

Great

Pedal

1. O God, we thank You for the gift of mu - sic's marv - 'lous strains;
2. We thank You for the in - spired minds that heard an in - ner song,
3. We thank You for the art - ists who, with skill of hand or voice,
4. We thank You for grand or - gans that a - wake the qui - et air.
5. Let ev - 'ry - thing with - in this world now make a joy - ful noise!

Its won - drous tunes have touched our souls, our low - ly lives are changed.
And set it then to staves with pen to pass it thus a - long.
In - ter - pret these great mel - o - dies and help our hearts re - joice.
Con - ceiv'd and built by art - i - sans whose work be - came their prayer.
Let ev - 'ry crea - ture that has breath lift heart, or hand, or voice!

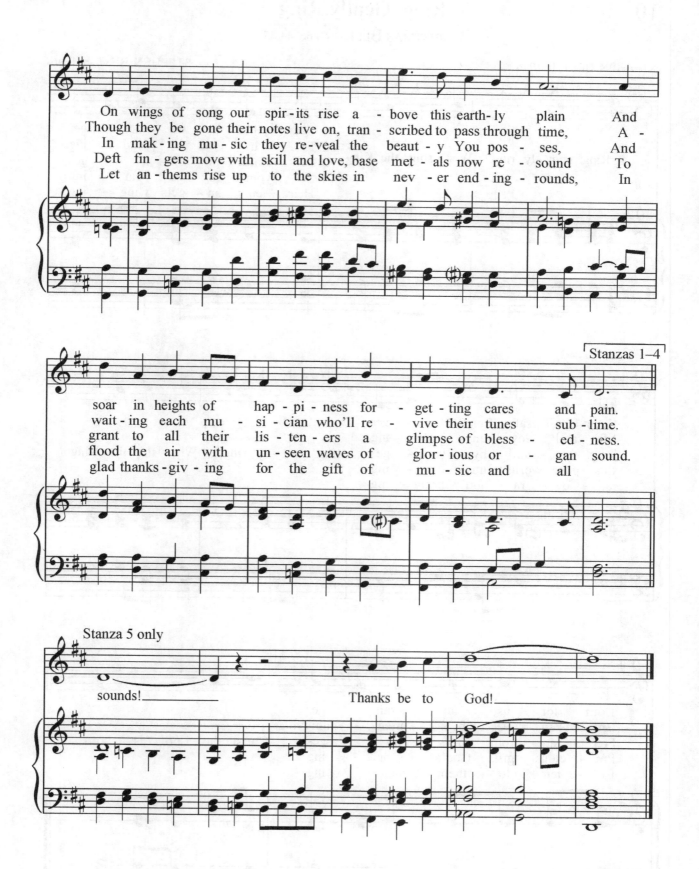

On wings of song our spir-its rise a - bove this earth-ly plain And
Though they be gone their notes live on, tran - scribed to pass through time, A -
In mak - ing mu-sic they re-veal the beaut-y You pos - ses, And
Deft fin - gers move with skill and love, base met - als now re - sound To
Let an -thems rise up to the skies in nev - er end-ing - rounds, In

Stanzas 1–4

soar in heights of hap-pi-ness for - get-ting cares and pain.
wait-ing each mu - si - cian who'll re - vive their tunes sub - lime.
grant to all their lis - ten-ers a glimpse of bless - ed - ness.
flood the air with un-seen waves of glor-ious or - gan sound.
glad thanks-giv-ing for the gift of mu - sic and all

Stanza 5 only

sounds!_____ Thanks be to God!_____

10   Ring, Gently Ring

CHRISTMAS BELLS   44 66. 44 65

STEPHEN BEST, b. 1946   STEPHEN BEST, b. 1946

Ring, gent-ly ring. Wor-ship the King.

1. See Him in the man - ger.
2. For us God is send - ing
3. Pro - mise of the a - ges,
4. So young to be bear - ing
5. Heav - en's an - gels wing - ing,

Keep Him safe from dan - ger.
life and joy un - end - ing.
long fore - told by sa - ges. Ring, gent-ly ring. Wor-ship the King.
this poor world's un - car - ing.
ad - o - ra - tion bring - ing.

Born for us, no stran - ger.
Bro - ken lives he's men - ding.
Free - ing from sin's wa - ges. Christ the Lord is born.
Pre - cious gift, God's shar - ing.
Lis - ten to their sing - ing:

Our Father in Heaven

THE LORD'S PRAYER 65 65. 65 65

SARAH J. HALE, 1788–1879

EDWARD MORRIS BOWMAN, 1848–1913

Keep Step with the Music of Union

NATIONAL HYMN

WILLIAM ROSS WALLACE, 1819–1881   GEORGE FREDERICK BRISTOW, 1825–1898

12

1. Keep step with the mu-sic of Un-ion, The mu-sic our an-ces-tors sung, When the States like a ju-bi-lant Chor-us, To glo-ri-ous sis-ter-hood sprung! Oh! Thus shall their great Con-sti-tu-tion, That guards all the homes, all the homes of the land,

2. Keep step with the mu-sic of Un-ion, What grand-eur its flag has un-rolled For the loy-al, a heav-en-wove rain-bow, For trait-tors a storm in each fold! The glor-ious shade of Mount Ver-non Still points, still points to each pa-triot grave, Still

3. Keep step with the mu-sic of Un-ion! The for-ests have sunk at its sound, The pi-o-neer's brows beam with tri-umph, And La-bor's broad op-u-lence crowned; Oh! Yet must all gi-ant rude for-ces Of Na-ture, of Na-ture be chained to our cars. All

moun - tain of free - dom and jus - tice, For mil - lions e - ter - nal - ly stand,
cries o'er the long might - y a - ges That Eag - le of Lex - ing - ton wave!
moun - tains, lakes, riv - ers and oc - eans Crouch un - der the Stripes and the Stars.

a Tempo

While we step to the mus - ic of U - nion, One Ban - ner a - bove o'er the sod___

One voice from A - mer - i - ca swell - ing, In wor - ship of Li - ber - ty's God.

4. Keep step with the music of Union,
   Thus still shall we nourish the light
Our fathers lit for the chained nations
   That darkle in Tyranny's night;
The blood of the whole world is with us,
   O'er ocean by Tyranny hurled,
And they who would dare to insult us
   Shall sink with the wrath of the world,
           CHORUS .

5. Keep step with the music of Union,
   The music of Liberty, Right;
Singing nations by brotherhood only
   Are bannered with honor and might.
Then hurrah for the Past with its glory!
   For the strong, earnest Present, hurrah!
And a cheer for the starry-browed Future
   With Freedom, and Virtue, and Law.
           CHORUS.

13   He Leadeth Me: O Blessed Thought

HE LEADETH ME   L. M., with Refrain

JOSEPH H. GILMORE, 1834–1918   WILLIAM B. BRADBURY, 1816–1868

1. He lead-eth me: O bless-ed thought! O words with heav'n-ly com-fort fraught!
2. Some-times 'mid scenes of deep-est gloom, Some-times where E - den's bow-ers bloom,
3. Lord, I would place my hand in Thine, Nor ev - er mur-mur nor re - pine;
4. And when my task on earth is done, When, by Thy grace, the vic-tory's won,

What - e'er I do, where - e'er I be, Still 'tis God's hand that lead - eth me.
By wa - ters still, o'er trou-bled sea, Still 'tis His hand that lead - eth me.
Con - tent, what - ev - er lot I see, Since 'tis my God that lead - eth me.
E'en death's cold wave I will not flee, Since God thro' Jor - dan lead - eth me.

He lead-eth me, He lead-eth me, By His own hand He lead-eth me:

His faith-ful fol-lower I would be, For by His hand He lead-eth me.

Lord of Our Life, and God of Our Salvation

ILIUM 11 11. 11 5

MATTHÄUS APPELES VON LÖWENSTERN, 1594–1648
Paraphrased by PHILLIP PUSEY, 1799–1855

DUDLEY BUCK, 1839–1909

1. Lord of our life, and God of our sal - va - tion, Star of our
2. See round Thine Ark the hung - ry bil - lows curl - ing! See how Thy
3. Lord, Thou canst help when earth - ly ar - mor fail - eth; Lord, Thou canst

night, and hope of ev - ery na - tion, Hear and re - ceive Thy
foes their ban - ners are un - furl - ing! Lord, while their darts en -
save when dead - ly sin as - sail - eth; Lord, o'er Thy Rock nor

Church -'s sup - pli - ca - tion, Lord God Al - might - y.
ven - om'd they are hurl - ing, Thou canst pre - serve us.
death nor hell pre - vail - eth; Grant us Thy peace, Lord!

15   If There's Anybody Here Like Weepin' Mary

WEEPIN' MARY   12 10. 12 10. 9 10

JOHN 20:1

SPIRITUAL
arr. HARRY T. BURLEIGH, 1866–1949

If there's an-y-bod-y here like weep-in' Ma-ry,
Call up-on your Je-sus, an' He'll draw nigh,
If there's an-y-bod-y here like weep-in' Ma-ry,
Call up-on your Je-sus, an' He'll draw nigh.
O,___ glo-ry, glo-ry hal-le-lu-jah!
Glo-ry be to my God, who rules on high!

I Bow My Forehead to the Dust

AMESBURY C. M. D.

JOHN GREENLEAF WHITTIER, 1807–1892

UZZIAH C. BURNAP, 1834–1900

1. I bow my fore-head to the dust, I veil mine eyes for shame,
2. Yet, in the mad-dening maze of things, And tossed by storm and flood,
3. I know not what the fu-ture hath Of mar-vel or sur-prise,
4. And so be-side the Si-lent Sea I wait the muf-fled oar;

And urge, in tremb-ling self-dis-trust, A prayer with-out a claim.
To one fixed stake my spir-it clings; I know that God is good.
As-sured a-lone that life and death His mer-cy un-der-lies.
No harm from him can come to me On o-cean or on shore.

I see the wrong that round me lies, I feel the guilt with-in;
I dim-ly guess from bless-ings known Of great-er out of sight,
And if my heart and flesh are weak To bear an un-tried pain,
I know not where his is-lands lift Their frond-ed palms in air:

I hear, with groan and tra-vail-cries, The world con-fess its sin.
And, with the chast-ened Psalm-ist, know His judg-ments too are right.
The bruis-ed reed he will not break, But strength-en and sus-tain.
I on-ly know I can-not drift Be-yond his love and care.

17   O Little Town of Bethlehem

St. Hilda   86 86. 76 86

PHILLIPS BROOKS, 1835–1893   WILLIAM SIDELL CHESTER, 1865–1900

1. O lit-tle town of Beth-le-hem! How still we see thee lie;
2. For Christ is born of Ma - ry; And gath-ered all a - bove,
3. How si-lent-ly, how si-lent-ly The won-drous Gift is giv'n!
4. O ho-ly Child of Beth-le-hem! De-scend to us, we pray;

A - bove thy deep and dream-less sleep The si-lent stars go by;
While mor-tals sleep, the an - gels keep Their watch of won-d'ring love.
So God im-parts to hu - man hearts The bless-ings of His heav'n.
Cast out our sin, and en - ter in, Be born in us to - day!

Yet in thy dark streets shin-eth The ev - er-last-ing Light;
O morn-ing stars, to-geth-er Pro - claim the ho - ly birth;
No ear may hear His com-ing, But in this world of sin,
We hear the Christ-mas an - gels The great glad tid-ings tell;

The hopes and fears of all the years Are met in Thee to - night.
And prais-es sing to God the King, And peace to all on earth.
Where meek souls will re - ceive Him still, The dear Christ en - ters in.
O come to us, a - bide with us, Our Lord, Im - man - u - el!

30

God Made Me for Himself

10 10. 10 10

HENRY W. BAKER, 1821–1877

KATE S. CHITTENDEN, 1856–1949

1. God made me for Himself, to serve Him here With love's pure
2. All need-ful grace was mine, thro' His dear Son, Whose life and
3. And I, poor sin - ner, cast it all a - way; Lived for the
4. O Ho - ly Spi - rit, with Thy fire di - vine, Melt in - to

ser - vice and in fil - ial fear; To show His praise; for
death, my full sal - va - tion won; Thy grace that would have
toil or pleas - ure of each day; As if no Christ had
tears this thank - less heart of mine; Teach me to love what

Him to la - bor now, Then see His glo - ry where the an - gels bow.
strength-en'd me, and taught Grace that would crown me when my work was wrought.
shed His pre - cious blood, As if I owed no hom - age to my God.
once I seemed to hate, And live to God, be - fore it be too late.

Praise Him, Ye Architects Who Planned

LAAST UNS ERFREUEN   88 44. 88, with Alleluias

CYRIL ARGENTINE ALINGTON, 1872–1955

Geistliche Kirchengesang Cologne 1623
Harm. RALPH VAUGHAN WILLIAMS, 1872–1958

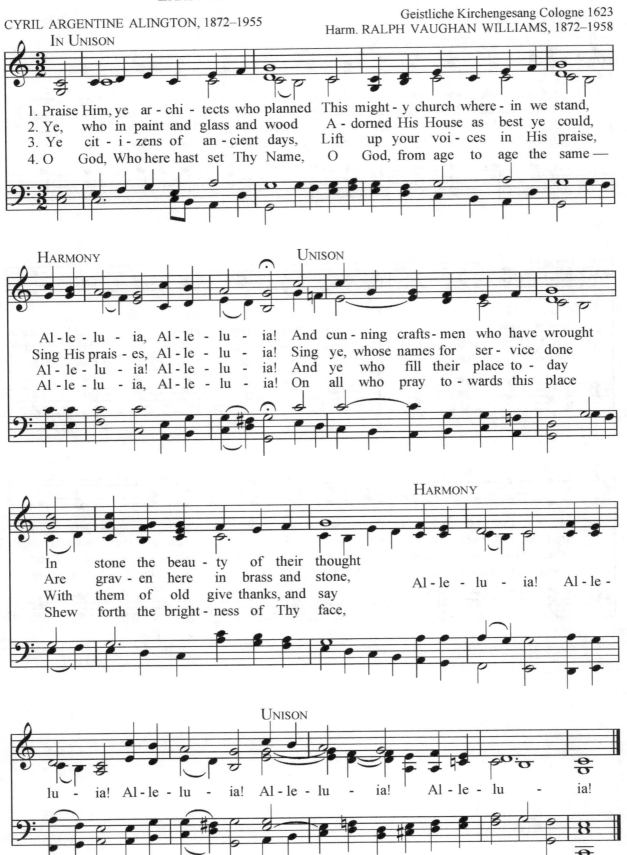

IN UNISON

1. Praise Him, ye ar - chi - tects who planned This might - y church where - in we stand,
2. Ye, who in paint and glass and wood A - dorned His House as best ye could,
3. Ye cit - i - zens of an - cient days, Lift up your voi - ces in His praise,
4. O God, Who here hast set Thy Name, O God, from age to age the same —

HARMONY   UNISON

Al - le - lu - ia, Al - le - lu - ia! And cun - ning crafts - men who have wrought
Sing His prais - es, Al - le - lu - ia! Sing ye, whose names for ser - vice done
Al - le - lu - ia! Al - le - lu - ia! And ye who fill their place to - day
Al - le - lu - ia, Al - le - lu - ia! On all who pray to - wards this place

HARMONY

In stone the beau - ty of their thought
Are grav - en here in brass and stone,   Al - le - lu - ia! Al - le -
With them of old give thanks, and say
Shew forth the bright - ness of Thy face,

UNISON

lu - ia! Al - le - lu - ia! Al - le - lu - ia! Al - le - lu - ia!

Pray, Without Ceasing, Pray!

Lenti S. M. D.

CHARLES WESLEY, 1707–1788

CARSON COOMAN, b. 1982

1. Pray, with-out ceas - ing, pray! Your Cap-tain gives the word.
2. In fel - low-ship, a - lone, To God with faith draw near,
3. Pour out your souls to God, And bow them with your knees,

His sum-mons cheer-ful - ly o - bey, And call up-on the Lord.
Ap-proach His courts, be - seige His throne With all the pow'rs of prayer:
And spread your hearts and hands a - broad, And pray for Zi - on's peace;

To God your ev - 'ry want In in - stant prayer dis - play;
Go to His tem - ple, go, Nor from His al - tar move;
Your guides and breth - ren bear For ev - er on your mind:

Pray al - ways; pray, and nev - er faint; Pray, with-out ceas - ing, pray.
Let ev - 'ry house His wor - ship know, And ev - 'ry heart His love.
Ex - tend the arms of might - y pray'r, In grasp-ing all man - kind.

The Son of God Goes Forth to War

ALL SAINTS, NEW C. M. D.

REGINALD HEBER, 1783–1826

HENRY STEPHEN CUTLER, 1824–1902

1. The Son of God goes forth to war, A king - ly crown to gain;
2. This mar - tyr first, whose ea - gle eye Could pierce be - yond the grave,
3. A glo - rious band, the cho - sen few On whom the Spir - it came,

His blood - red ban - ner streams a - far: Who fol - lows in His train?
Who saw his Mas - ter in the sky, And called on Him to save:
Twelve val - iant saints, their hope they knew, And mocked the cross and flame;

Who best can drink His cup of woe, Tri - umph - ant o - ver pain,
Like Him, with par - don on His tongue, In midst of mor - tal pain,
They climbed the steep as - cent of heav'n Thro' per - il, toil, and pain:

Who pa - tient bears His cross be - low, He fol - lows in His train.
He prayed for them that did the wrong: Who fol - lows in His train?
O God, to us may grace be giv'n To fol - low in their train!

Sweetly the Birds Are Singing

AN EASTER CAROL 74 74. 64, with Refrain

22

EMILY D. CHAPMAN

LEOPOLD DAMROSCH, 1832–1885

23 O Lord, Our God, Thy Mighty Hand

PEACE-HYMN OF THE REPUBLIC 77 66. 77 66

HENRY VAN DYKE. 1852–1933   WALTER DAMROSCH, 1862–1950

With stately rhythm

1. O   Lord, our God, Thy might - y hand Hath made our coun - try free;
2. The strength of ev - 'ry state in - crease In Un - ion's gold - en chain;
3. O   suf - fer not her feet to stray; But guide her un - taught might,
4. Through all the wait - ing land pro - claim Thy gos - pel of good - will;

From all her broad and hap - py land May praise a - rise to Thee.
Her thou - sand cit - ies fill with peace, Her mil - lion fields with grain.
That she may walk in peace - ful day, And lead the world in light.
And may the mu - sic of Thy name In ev - 'ry bos - om thrill.

Ful - fill the pro - mise of her youth, Her lib - er - ty de - fend;
The vir - tues of her ming - led blood In one new peo - ple blend;
Bring down the proud, lift up the poor, Un - e - qual ways a - mend;
O'er hill and vale, from sea to sea, Thy ho - ly reign ex - tend;

By law and or - der, love and truth,
By un - i - ty and broth - er - hood,   A - mer - i - ca be - friend!
By jus - tice, nation - wide and sure,
By faith and hope and char - i - ty,

To Samuel M. Shoemaker

All the Past We Leave Behind

GRAMERCY 78 88. 87

24

WALT WHITMAN, 1818–1892

VERNON DE TAR, 1905–1999

1. All the past we leave be-hind, We take up the task e-ter-nal, and the
2. Not for de-lec-ta-tions sweet, Not the rich-es safe and pall-ing, not for
3. All the pul-ses of the world, All the joy-ous, all the sor-rowing, these are
4. On and on the com-pact ranks, With ac-cess-ions ev-er wait-ing, we must

bur-den, and the les-son, Con-que'ring, hold-ing, dar-ing, ven-tur-ing
us the tame en-joy ment; Nev-er must you be di-vi-ded,
of us, they are with us, We to-day's pro-cess-ion head-ing,
nev-er yield or fal-ter, Through the bat-tle Thro' de-feat,___

Sopranos ad lib.

so we go the un-known ways,___
in our ranks you move u-nit-ed, Pi - o - neers! O Pi - o - neers!
we the route for tra-vel clear-ing,
mov-ing yet and nev-er stop-ping,

25 Goin' Home

Largo, Symphony No. 9, "From the New World"

WILLIAM ARMS FISHER, 1861–1948   ANTONIN DVOŘÁK, 1841–1904

1. Go - in' home, go - in' home, I'm a - go - in' home; Qui - et - like, some still day, I'm just go - in' home. It's not far, just close by, Thru an o - pen door; Work all done, care laid by, goin' to fear no more. Moth - er's there ex - pect - ing me Fa - ther's wait - in' too; Lots o' folk gath - er'd there, All the friends I knew.

2. Morn - in' star lights the way, Res'-less dream all done; Shad-ows gone, break o' day, Real life jes' be - gun. There's no break, there's no end, Jes' a - liv - in' on, Wide a - wake, with a smile, Go - in' on and on. Go - in' home, go - in' home, I'm jes' go - in' home; It's not far, jes' close by Thru an o - pen door.

FINE

No - thin' lost, all's gain, No more fret nor pain, No more stum-blin' on the way

No more long-in' for the day, Goin' to roam no more!

Savior, Breathe an Evening Blessing 26

ORISON 87 87

JAMES EDMESTON, 1791–1867

CLARENCE DICKINSON, 1873–1969

1. Sav - ior, breathe an eve - ning bless - ing, Ere re - pose our spir - its seal;
2. Though de - struc - tion walk a - round us, Though the ar - rows past us fly,
3. Though the night be dark and drear - y, Dark - ness can - not hide from Thee;
4. Should swift death this night o'er - take us, And our couch be - come our tomb,

Sin and want we come con - fess - ing; Thou canst save, and Thou canst heal.
An - gel guards from Thee sur - round us: We are safe, if Thou art nigh.
Thou art He who, nev - er wea - ry, Watch - est where Thy peo - ple be.
May the morn in heav'n a - wake us, Clad in light and death - less bloom.

27 In Zion's Sacred Gates

CURTIS 66 66. 88

TIMOTHY DWIGHT, 1752–1817

ALFRED V. FEDAK, b. 1953

1. In Zi - on's sa - cred gates, Let hymns of praise be - gin,
2. The trum - pet's mar - tial voice, The tim - brel's soft - er sound,
3. Re - joice! our Lord is King! Our God and King a - dore;

Where acts of faith and love In cease - less beau - ty shine:
The or - gan's sol - emn peal, His prais - es shall re - sound:
Yea, all give thanks and sing, And tri - umph ev - er - more;

In mer - cy there, while God is known, Be - fore His throne with songs ap - pear.
To swell the song, with high - est joy Let man em - ploy His tune - ful tongue.
Lift up the heart, Lift up the voice, Re - joice a - loud, Let all re - joice.

Now, on Land and Sea Descending

CHANGELESS LOVE 87 87

SAMUEL LONGFELLOW, 1819–1892

CARYL FLORIO, 1843–1920

1. Now, on land and sea descending, Brings to night its peace profound,
2. Now, our wants and burdens leaving To His care, who cares for all,

Let our vesper hymn be blending With the holy calm around.
Cease we fearing, cease we grieving; At His touch our burdens fall.

Soon as dies the sunset's glory Stars of heav'n shine out above,
As the darkness deepens o'er us, Lo! eternal stars arise;

Telling still the ancient story— Their Creator's changeless love.
Hope, and faith, and love rise glorious, Shining in the Spirit's skies.

29   What Did Our Lord and Saviour Say

SUFFER LITTLE CHILDREN 89, with Refrain

STEPHEN COLLINS FOSTER, 1826–1864   STEPHEN COLLINS FOSTER, 1826–1864

DUET *Asks the Questions.*

1. What did our Lord and Sav-iour say When oth-ers wished to drive us a-way?
2. What did He say who from a-bove Came down to teach us kind-ness and love?
3. What were the words of Him who bled, Nailed to the cross with thorns on His head?
4. What did He say whose Spir-it shed Hope to the liv-ing, life to the dead?
5. If on His mer-cy we re-ly, What will His words be when we die?

Inst.

CHORUS *Answers them.*

"Suf-fer lit-tle child-ren to come un-to me, Of such is the king-dom of heav'n.

30   Our Flag above the Clouds Is Ever Waving Free

THE FLAG 86 86. 86 86, with Referain

JOEL LEWIS   HENRY HADLEY, 1871–1937

Moderato and majestic ♩ = 92

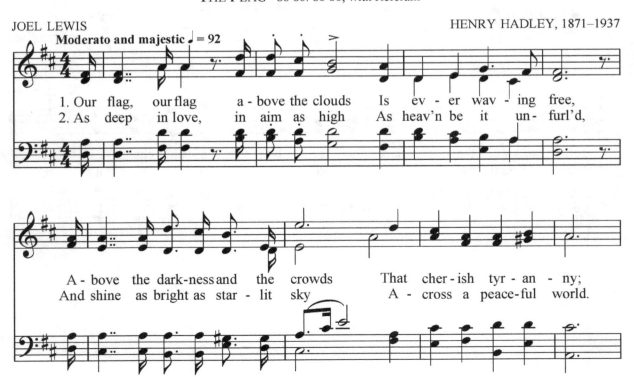

1. Our flag, our flag a-bove the clouds Is ev-er wav-ing free,
2. As deep in love, in aim as high As heav'n be it un-furl'd,

A-bove the dark-ness and the crowds That cher-ish tyr-an-ny;
And shine as bright as star-lit sky A-cross a peace-ful world.

42

And may it long be like its stars A com-fort and a light, To
And wide in char - i - ty and good As sun-shine may it be, The

dim. *rit.*

na - tions dark with sin and care, To them that sit in night.
flag of hu - man broth - er - hood, Of Right and Lib - er - ty.

that sit in night.
and Lib - er - ty.

f a tempo.

Our flag that hath the fires of heav'n; The sun-set's glow, the free blue sea;

mf *cresc.* *f*

The might - y sym - bols of the soul, The glo - ry of hu - man - i - ty.

31   All Glory to God

TOLAND   11 10. 10 10. 12 12

SEBASTIAN M. GLÜCK, b. 1960
harm. DANIEL E. SCHWANDT, b. 1977

SEBASTIAN M. GLÜCK, b. 1960

1. All glo-ry to God, praise Him in His tem-ple
2. Ex-alt Him with song and blasts of the sho-far
3. A life-time of grace shall weld us to-geth-er,

Be-neath the great vault of heav-en ex-alt
With fac-ile com-mand of pipe or-gans grand
E-ter-nal the flame with free-dom from shame.

With truth as our tool that know-ledge may rule
That shak-eth the ground as tem-ples re-sound
The mind as the force that fol-lows the course

So like as a-bove and so, too, be-low
With cym-bals' loud crash de-spair do we smash
His per-fect de-sign for-ev-er must shine,

Our wis - dom, our love shall the dark - ness ov - er - throw
Let mus - ic bring cheer for hu - man - i - ty to hear
Re - flect - ing the call of the arch - i - tect of all,

Our wis - dom, our love shall the dark - ness ov - er - throw.
Let mus - ic bring cheer for hu - man - i - ty to hear.
Re - flect - ing the call of the arch - i - tect of all.

We Thank Thee for That Precious Word

32

ISAAC S. MOSES, 1847–1926   THE PRECIOUS WORD 887 887

GIDEON FROELICH, b. ca. 1846

We thank Thee for that pre - cious word, The truth Thou hast on us con - ferr'd,

It is sal - va - tion's por tal, Thy pre - cepts an - swer ev - 'ry need,

Through peace - ful pas - tures, Lord, they lead, To light and life im - mor - tal.

33 At the Name of Jesus Ev'ry Knee Shall Bow

BAVARIA 65 65. D.

CAROLINE MARIA NOEL, 1817–1877

CLEMENT R. GALE, 1862–1937

mf

1. At the Name of Je - sus Ev - 'ry knee shall bow,
2. At His voice cre - a - tion Sprang at once to sight,
3. Hum - bled for a sea - son, To re - ceive a Name
4. Bro - thers, this Lord Je - sus Shall re - turn a - gain,

Ev - 'ry tongue con - fess Him King of Glo - ry now;
All the an - gel fac - es, All the hosts of light,
From the lips of sin - ners, Un - to whom He came,
With His Fa - ther's glo - ry, With His an - gel train;

'Tis the Fa - ther's pleas - ure We should call Him Lord,
Thrones and Dom - in - a - tions, Stars up - on their way,
Faith - ful - ly He bore it Spot - less to the last,
For all wreaths of em - pire Meet up - on His brow,

Who from the be - gin - ning Was the might - y Word.
All the heav - 'nly Or - ders, In their great ar - ray.
Brought it back vic - to - rious, When from death He passed;
And our hearts con - fess Him King of Glo - ry now.

The Earth Is Full of Joyful Praise

THIS HAPPY CHRISTMAS MORNING   87 87. 88 87

34

IDA SCOTT TAYLOR, 1855–1932

S. ARCHER GIBSON, 1875–1952

1. The earth is full of joy-ful praise,
2. The bells the notes of joy re-peat, This hap-py Christ-mas morn-ing,
3. Ho-san-nas swell from near and far,

To cel-e-brate the day of days,
They chime in mea-sures glad and sweet, This hap-py Christ-mas morn-ing:
Their theme is Je-sus and His Star,

The Lord is born! oh hear the cry That rings in tri-umph thro' the sky!
The sound-ing seas are tuned to song, The isles ring out, ten thou-sand strong,
A tide of song is in the air, The Sav-iour's ad-vent to de-clare,

All praise to God who reigns on high,
The Sav-iour's glo-ry to pro long, This hap-py Christ-mas morn-ing!
And there is glad-ness ev-'ry-where

Away in a Manger

CHRISTMAS LULLABYE 11 11. 11 11

ANONYMOUS   ARCHER GIBSON, 1875–1952

1. A - way in a man - ger, no crib for a bed,
2. The cat - tle are low - ing, the poor ba - by wakes,
3. Be near me, Lord Je - sus, I ask Thee to stay

The lit - tle Lord Je - sus laid down His sweet head.
But lit - tle Lord Je - sus, no cry - ing He makes.
Close by me for - ev - er, and love me, I pray.

The stars in the heav - ens looked down where He lay, The
I love Thee, Lord Je - sus! Look down from the sky, And
Bless all the dear chil - dren in Thy ten - der care, And

lit - tle Lord Je - sus a - sleep on the hay, The
stay by my cra - dle till morn - ing is nigh, And
take us to heav - en to live with Thee there. And

lit - tle Lord Je - sus a - sleep on the hay.
stay by my cra - dle till morn - ing is nigh.
take us to heav - en to live with Thee there.

Awake, Awake to Love and Work

86 86. D.

GEOFFREY A. STUDDERT KENNEDY, 1883–1929

PERCY ALDRIDGE GRAINGER, 1882–1961

1. A - wake, a - wake to love and work, The lark is in the sky,
2. Come let thy voice be one with theirs, Shout with their shout of praise;
3. To give and give, and give a - gain, What God hath giv - en thee;

The fields are wet with dia - mond dew, The worlds a - wake to cry
See how the gi - ant sun soars up, Great lord of years and days!
To spend thy - self nor count the cost, To serve right glo - rious - ly

Their bless - ings on the Lord of Life, As He goes meek - ly by.
So let the love of Je - sus come And set thy soul a - blaze:
The God who gave all worlds that are, And all that are to be.

Their bless - ings on the Lord of Life, As He goes meek - ly by.
So let the love of Je - sus come And set thy soul a - blaze:
The God who gave all worlds that are, And all that are to be.

37

Holy Spirit, Truth Divine

MERCY 77 77

SAMUEL LONGFELLOW, 1819–1892

LOUIS MOREAU GOTTSCHALK, 1829–1869

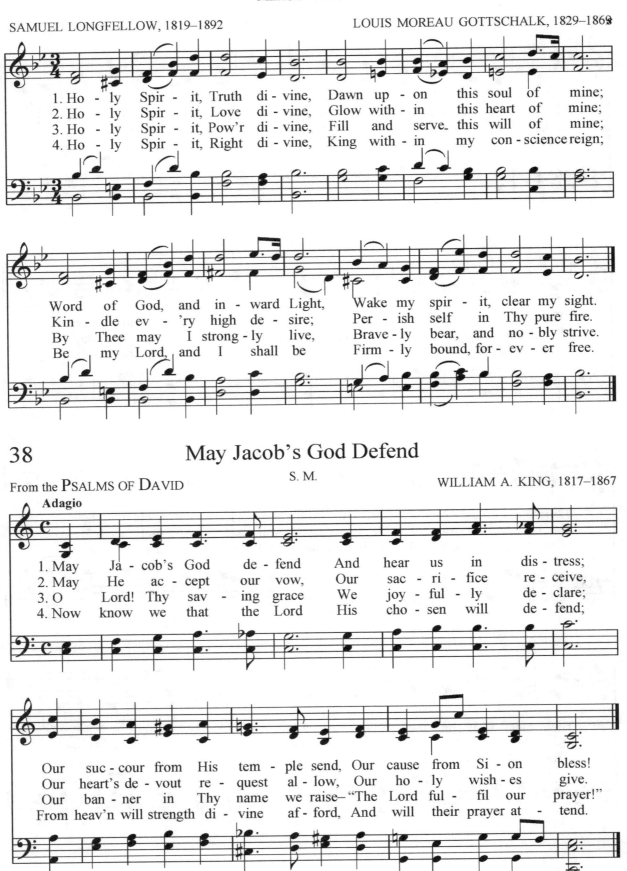

1. Ho - ly Spir - it, Truth di - vine, Dawn up - on this soul of mine;
2. Ho - ly Spir - it, Love di - vine, Glow with - in this heart of mine;
3. Ho - ly Spir - it, Pow'r di - vine, Fill and serve this will of mine;
4. Ho - ly Spir - it, Right di - vine, King with - in my con - science reign;

Word of God, and in - ward Light, Wake my spir - it, clear my sight.
Kin - dle ev - 'ry high de - sire; Per - ish self in Thy pure fire.
By Thee may I strong - ly live, Brave - ly bear, and no - bly strive.
Be my Lord, and I shall be Firm - ly bound, for - ev - er free.

38

May Jacob's God Defend

S. M.

From the PSALMS OF DAVID

WILLIAM A. KING, 1817–1867

Adagio

1. May Ja - cob's God de - fend And hear us in dis - tress;
2. May He ac - cept our vow, Our sac - ri - fice re - ceive,
3. O Lord! Thy sav - ing grace We joy - ful - ly de - clare;
4. Now know we that the Lord His cho - sen will de - fend;

Our suc - cour from His tem - ple send, Our cause from Si - on bless!
Our heart's de - vout re - quest al - low, Our ho - ly wish - es give.
Our ban - ner in Thy name we raise–"The Lord ful - fil our prayer!"
From heav'n will strength di - vine af - ford, And will their prayer at - tend.

How Bless'd Are They Who Always Keep

BORNE C. M.

From PSALM 119
TATE & BRADY, 1698

HENRY W. GREATOREX, 1811–1858

1. How bless'd are they who always keep The pure and perfect way; Who nev-er from the sa-cred paths Of God's com-mand-ments stray!
2. Thrice bless'd! who to his right-eous laws Have still o-bed-ient been; And have with fer-vent, hum-ble zeal His fa-vor sought to win.
3. Thou strict-ly hast en-joined us, Lord, To learn Thy sa-cred will, And all our di-li-gence em-ploy Thy stat-utes to ful-fil.
4. O then that Thy most ho-ly will Might o'er my ways pre-side, And I the course of all my life By Thy di-rec-tion guide!
5. Then with as-sur-ance should I walk, From all con-fu-sion free, Con-vinced with joy that all my ways With Thy com-mands a-gree.

Adam Lay Ybounden

65 55. 66 55. 68 55

MIDDLE ENGLISH, ca. 1400

FREDERICK GRIMES, b. 1941

Am I a Soldier of the Cross

PENNSYLVANIA C. M. D.

ISAAC WATTS, 1674–1748

FRANK SEYMOUR HASTINGS, 1853–1924

1. Am I a sol - dier of the cross, A fol - low'r of the Lamb?
2. Are there no foes for me to face? Must I not stem the flood?
3. Thy saints in all this glo - rious war Shall con - quer, tho' they die;

And shall I fear to own His cause, Or blush to speak His Name?
Is this vile world a friend to grace, To help me on to God?
They see the tri - umph from a - far, By faith they bring it nigh.

Must I be car - ried to the skies On flow - 'ry beds of ease,
Sure I must fight, if I would reign: In - crease my cour - age, Lord;
When that il - lus - trious day shall rise, And all Thy arm - ies shine

While oth - ers fought to win the prize, And sail'd thro' blood - y seas?
I'll bear the toil, en - dure the pain, Sup - port - ed by Thy word.
In robes of vic - t'ry thro' the skies, The glo - ry shall be Thine.

42 Rock of Ages, Cleft for Me

TOPLADY 77 77. 77

AUGUSTUS M. TOPLADY, 1740–1778, alt.

THOMAS HASTINGS, 1784–1872

1. Rock of A - ges, cleft for me, Let me hide my - self in Thee;
2. Could my tears for - ev - er flow, Could my zeal no lan - gour know,
3. While I draw this fleet - ing breath, When my eyes shall close in death,

Let the wa - ter and the blood, From Thy wound - ed side which flowed,
These for sin could not a - tone; Thou must save, and Thou a - lone;
When I rise to worlds un - known, And be - hold Thee on Thy throne;

Be of sin the dou - ble cure, Save from wrath and make me pure.
In my hand no price I bring; Sim - ply to Thy cross I cling.
Rock of A - ges, cleft for me, Let me hide my - self in Thee.

Break New-Born Year

BRISTOL C. M.

THOMAS HORNBLOWER GILL, 1819–1906

EDWARD HODGES, 1796–1867

43

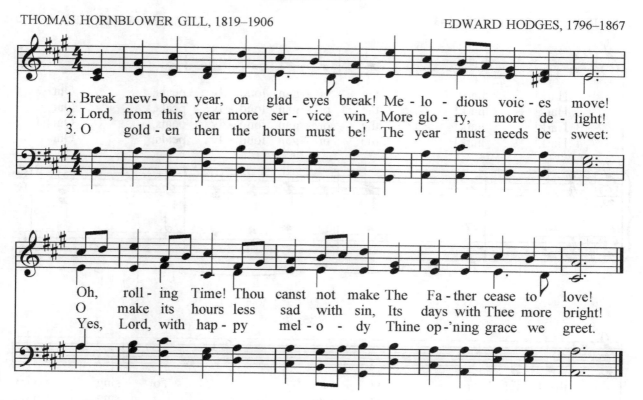

1. Break new-born year, on glad eyes break! Me-lo-dious voic-es move!
2. Lord, from this year more ser-vice win, More glo-ry, more de-light!
3. O gold-en then the hours must be! The year must needs be sweet:

Oh, roll-ing Time! Thou canst not make The Fa-ther cease to love!
O make its hours less sad with sin, Its days with Thee more bright!
Yes, Lord, with hap-py mel-o-dy Thine op-'ning grace we greet.

Bread of the World, in Mercy Broken

EUCHARISTIC HYMN 98 98

REGINALD HEBER, 1783–1836

JOHN S.B. HODGES, 1830–1915

44

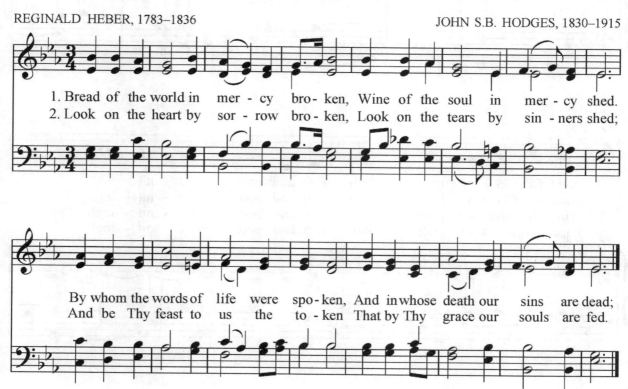

1. Bread of the world in mer-cy bro-ken, Wine of the soul in mer-cy shed.
2. Look on the heart by sor-row bro-ken, Look on the tears by sin-ners shed;

By whom the words of life were spo-ken, And in whose death our sins are dead;
And be Thy feast to us the to-ken That by Thy grace our souls are fed.

45   Hark! Hark! The Organ Loudly Peals

AN ORGAN HYMN   87 87. 66 66. 7

GODFREY THRING, 1823–1903   DAVID HURD, b. 1950

1. Hark! hark! the or-gan loud-ly peals, Our thank-ful hearts in-vit-ing To sing our great Cre-a-tor's praise, Both rich and poor u-nit-ing!

2. Hark! hark! the or-gan loud-ly peals, Our thank-ful hearts in-vit-ing To sing the praise of Christ our King, Both rich and poor u-nit-ing!

3. Hark! hark! the or-gan loud-ly peals, Our thank-ful hearts in-vit-ing To sing the Ho-ly Spir-it's praise, Both rich and poor u-nit-ing!

4. Hark! hark! the or-gan loud-ly peals, Our thank-ful hearts in-vit-ing To high up-raise our songs of praise, Both rich and poor u-nit-ing!

Not in Dumb Resignation

CASTELAR P. M.

JOHN JAY, 1838–1905   HENRY HOLDEN HUSS, 1862–1953

1. Not in dumb res - ig - na - tion, We lift our hands on high;
2. When ty - rant feet are tramp - ling Up - on the com - mon weal,
3. Thy will! it bids the weak be strong; It bids the strong be just:

Not like the nerve - less fa - tal - ist, Con - tent to do and die.
Thou dost not bid us bend and writhe Be - neath the iron heel.
No lip to fawn, no hand to beg, No brow to seek the dust.

Our faith springs like the ea - gle's, Who soars to meet the sun,
In Thy name we as - sert our right By sword, or tongue, or pen,
Where - ev - er man op - press - es man Be - neath the lib - 'ral sun,

And cries ex - ult - ing un - to Thee, "O Lord, Thy will be done."
And ev'n the heads - man's axe may flash Thy mes - sage un - to men.
O Lord, be there, Thine arm made bare, Thy right - eous will be done.

O Master of the Desert Place

BREAD OF THE DESERT 88 88. 88

JOSEPH ADDISON RICHARDS, 1858–1928

DION W. KENNEDY, 1882–1946

47

1. O Mas-ter of the des-ert place, Where throngs were great and loaves were few,
2. O Mas-ter of the des-ert hill, Where Sin re-ceived His prom-ised wage,
3. O Mas-ter of the men who fed Five thou-sand in a des-ert place,
4. O Mas-ter of the des-ert place, That soon shall blos-som at the rose,

An-gel-ic ser-vants of Thy grace Once scat-tered man-na in the dew.
A corn of wheat there died, to fill The world with bread from age to age.
With-in their hands five loaves of bread Were mul-ti-plied by Thy great grace.
The laugh-ing sea-sons then will chase With fruits each la-bor-er that sows.

With-in the dew of prayer may we The dai-ly bread of heav-en see.
O Sav-iour Christ, help us to take God's loaf, there bro-ken for our sake.
Help us to fear no des-ert lands Since Thou art bread with-in our hands.
The glo-ry of that day we sing When God His har-vest home shall bring.

48 Ancient of Days, Who Sittest Throned in Glory

ANCIENT OF DAYS 11 10. 11 10

WILLIAM C. DOANE, 1832–1913

J. ALBERT JEFFERY, 1855–1929

1. An-cient of Days, Who sit-test, thron'd in glo-ry;
2. O Ho - ly Fa - ther, who hast led Thy chil-dren
3. O Ho - ly Je - sus, Prince of Peace and Sav-iour,
4. O Ho - ly Ghost, the Lord and the Life Giv- er,
5. O Tri - une God, with heart and voice a - dor-ing,

Alla mæstosa progressione ♪ = 100

To Thee all knees are   bent, all voic- es pray;   Thy love has bless'd the
In all the a - ges,   with the fire and cloud,   Thro' seas dry - shod, through
To Thee we owe the   peace that still pre-vails,   Still - ing the rude wills
Thine is the quick-'ning   pow'r that gives in-crease;   From Thee have flowed, as
Praise we the good-ness   that doth crown our days;   Pray we that Thou wilt

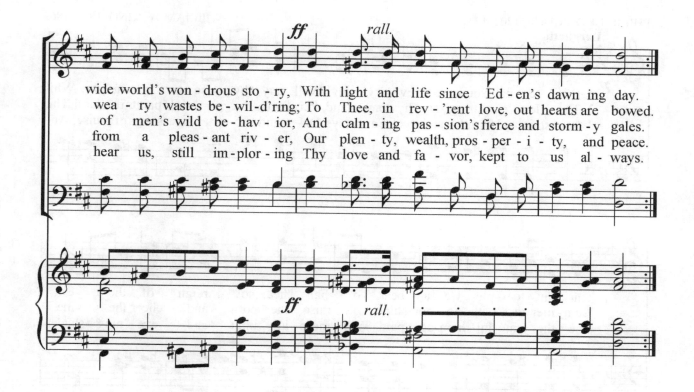

wide world's won-drous sto-ry, With light and life since Ed-en's dawn ing day.
wea-ry wastes be-wil-d'ring; To Thee, in rev-'rent love, out hearts are bowed.
of men's wild be-hav-ior, And calm-ing pas-sion's fierce and storm-y gales.
from a pleas-ant riv-er, Our plen-ty, wealth, pros-per-i-ty, and peace.
hear us, still im-plor-ing Thy love and fa-vor, kept to us al-ways.

Hope of the World

From among 500 ecumenical hymns submitted, this by
Georgia Harkness (1891–1974) of the faculty of Pacific
School of Religion, Berkeley, Calif., was selected as best.
The hymns were written in honor of the Second World
Council of Churches Assembly that met in Evanston, Ill.,
in August 1954.

1. Hope of the world, Thou Christ of great compassion
   Speak to our fearful hearts by conflict rent.
   Save us, Thy people, fron consuming passion,
   Who by our own false hopes and aims are spent.

2. Hope of the world, God's gift from highest heaven,
   Bringing to hungry souls the bread of life.
   Still let Thy spirit unto us be given
   To heal earth's wounds and end her bitter strife.

3. Hope of the world, afoot on dusty highways,
   Showing to wandering souls the path of light;
   Walk Thou beside us lest the tempting byways
   Lure us away from Thee to endless night.

4. Hope of the world, who by Thy cross didst save us
   From death and dark despair, from sin and guilt,
   We render back the love Thy mercy gave us;
   Take Thou our lives and use them as Thou wilt.

49   Eternal Source of Every Joy!

L. M.

PHILIP DODDRIDGE, 1702–1751   WILLIAM A. KING, 1817–1867

1. E - ter-nal Source of ev-'ry joy! Well may Thy praise our lips em-ploy, While in Thy tem-ple we ap-pear, To hail Thee, sov'-reign of the year, Wide as the wheels of na-ture roll, Thy hand sup-ports and guides the whole, The sun is taught by Thee to rise, And dark-ness when to veil the skies.

2. The flow-'ry spring, at Thy com-mand, Per-fumes the air and paints the land; The sum-mer rays with vi-gor shine To raise the corn and cheer the vine. Thy hand, in au-tumn, rich-ly pours Thro' all our coasts re-dun-dant stores; While win-ter's, soft-en'd by Thy care, No face of want or hor-or wear.

3. Sea-sons, and months, and weeks, and days De-mand suc-ces-sive songs of praise; And be the grate-ful hom-age paid, With morn-ing light, and eve-'ning shade, Here in Thy house let in-cense rise, And cir-cling sab-baths bless our eyes, 'Till to those bright-er courts we soar, Where days and years re-volve no more.

By Thy Thirst at Jacob's Well

LIBERA NOS, DOMINE 77 77. 77, with Refrain

The Irish Messenger

BRUNO OSCAR KLEIN, 1858–1911

Adagio

1. By Thy thirst at Ja-cob's well, Thirst that words can nev - er tell,
2. By Thy sad and si - lent gaze On the griefs of these our days,
3. Youth, and age, and man-hood cry To Thy Heart en-throned on high.
4. By Thy thirst on Cal - va - ry, Lov - ing Sav - iour, set us free

Parch - èd lips and parch - èd tongue, And Thy Heart, so sore - ly wrung
Blight - ed hearts and blight - ed homes, All the ag - o - ny that comes
We are weak, but Thou art strong, Lord and we have suf - fered long—
From the thral - dom of this sin, Sav - iour, let Thy parch'd lips win

With the thought of fu - ture years, Of our sor - rows, of our tears—
From the dark, hot fount of woe, Par - don us who suf - fer so—
Raise the weight of pain we bear, Thou, our Mak - er, hear our prayer—
Grace, and peace, and con - q'ring strength, Sav - iour, hear our cry at length—

Li - be - ra nos, Do - mi - ne, Li - be - ra nos, Do - mi - ne.

51   Blessed Assurance

ASSURANCE   9 10. 99, with Refrain

FANNY J. CROSBY, 1820–1915   PHOEBE PALMER KNAPP, 1839–1908

1. Bless-ed as-sur-ance, Je-sus is mine! O what a fore-taste of glo-ry di-vine!
2. Per-fect sub-mis-sion, per-fect de-light, vi-sions of rap-ture now burst on my sight;
3. Per-fect sub-mis-sion, all is at rest; I in my Sav-ior am hap-py and blest,

Heir of sal-va-tion, pur-chase of God, born of His Spir-it, washed in His blood.
an-gels de-scend-ing bring from a-bove ech-oes of mer-cy, whis-pers of love.
watch-ing and wait-ing, look-ing a-bove, filled with His good-ness, lost in His love.

REFRAIN

This is my sto-ry, this is my song, prais-ing my Sav-ior all the day long;

this is my sto-ry, this is my song, prais-ing my Sav-ior all the day long.

God of Our Fathers, Known of Old

RECESSIONAL 88 88. 88

RUDYARD KIPLING, 1865–1936

REGINALD DE KOVEN, 1859–1920

Allegro mæstoso

1. God of our fa - thers, known of old, Lord of our far - flung bat - tle line,
2. The tu - mult and the shout - ing dies, The Cap - tains and the Kings de - part.
3. Far call'd our na - vies melt a - way On dune and head - land sinks the fire
4. If drunk with sight of pow'r we loose Wild tongues that have not Thee in awe,
5. For heath - en heart that puts her trust In reek - ing tube and i - ron shard,

Be - neath whose aw - ful hand we hold Do - min - ion o - ver palm and pine:
Still stands thine an - cient sac - ri - fice An hum - ble and a con - trite heart,
Lo, all our pomp of yes - ter - day Is one with Nin - e - veh and Tyre!
Such boast - ing as the Gen - tiles use, Or les - ser breeds with - out the law,
All val - iant dust that builds on dust, And guard - ing calls not Thee to guard.

Lord God of Hosts, be with us yet,
Lord God of Hosts, be with us yet,
Judge of the na - tions, spare us yet,
Lord God of Hosts, be with us yet,
For fran - tic boast and fool - ish word, Thy mer - cy on Thy peo ple, Lord!

Lest we for - get, lest we for - get.

Shall We Gather at the River

HANSON PLACE 87 87, with Refrain

ROBERT LOWRY, 1826–1899   ROBERT LOWRY, 1826–1899

Cheerful

1. Shall we gath - er at the riv - er. Where bright an - gel feet have trod,
2. On the mar - gin of the riv - er, Wash - ing up its sil - ver spray,
3. On the bos - om of the riv - er, Where the Sav - ior-king we own,___
4. Ere we reach the shin - ing riv - er, Lay we ev - 'ry bur - den down:
5. At the smil - ing of the riv - er, Mir - or of the Sav - ior's face,*__
6. Soon we'll reach the shin - ing riv - er, Soon our pil - grim - age will cease;

With its crys - tal tide for ev - er, Flow - ing by the throne of God?
We will walk and wor - ship ev - er, All the hap - py gold - en day.
We shall meet, and sor - row nev - er, 'Neath the glo - ry of the throne.
Grace our spir - its will de - liv - er, And pro - vide a robe and crown.
Saints, whom death will nev - er sev - er, Lift their songs of sav - ing grace.
Soon our hap - py hearts will quiv - er With the mel - o - dy of peace.

CHORUS

Yes, we'll gath - er at the riv - er, The beau - ti - ful, the beau - ti - ful riv - er,

Gath - er with the saints at the riv - er That flows by the throne of God.

*Many early versions had "Rippling with the Savior's face."

Because Thy Trust Is God Alone

MARTHINA L. M.

The Psalter, 1912

J. CHRISTOPHER MARKS, 1863–1946

1. Be - cause thy trust is God a - lone, Thy ref - uge
2. An - gel - ic guards at His com - mands Will bear thee
3. Tho' fierce and treach - 'rous foes as - sail, Their pow'r and
4. Com - plete de - liv - 'rance I will give, And hon - or

is the High - est One, No e - vil shall up -
safe - ly in their hands, Will keep thee, lest, if
wrath shall not pre - vail; Their cru - el strength, their
him while he shall live; A - bun - dant life I

on thee come, Nor plague ap - proach thy guard - ed home.
left a - lone, Thou dash thy foot a - gainst a stone.
ven - om'd spite, Thou shalt o'er - come with con - quering might.
will be - stow, To him My full sal - va - tion show.

54

55 Sing with Joyful Acclamation

CHRIST THE LORD IS BORN 85 85. 88 85, with Refrain

IDA SCOTT TAYLOR, 1885–1932

WILL C. MACFARLANE, 1870–1945

Brightly, but not too fast

1. Sing with joy-ful ac-cla-ma-tion, Christ the Lord is born!
2. Shine on, O sun, in roy-al splen-dor,
3. Sons of Zi-on, bow be-fore Him,

Let it sound thro' all cre-a-tion, Christ the Lord is born!
Waft, O breeze, the mes-sage ten-der,
With en-rap-tured sons a-dore Him,

Shout a-loud, ye moun-tains hoar-y, Wel-come to the King of Glo-ry,
Tell it out, ye waves of o-cean, Thrill-ing with a glad com-mo-tion,
Christ is born, sal-va-tion bring-ing, Theme to set the joy-bells ring-ing,

Tell to earth the wond-rous sto - ry,
Thun - der forth in deep de - vo - tion— Christ the Lord is born!
Theme to set our tongues to sing - ing,—

CHORUS

A little slower

Hal - le - lu - jah! an - gels say, Christ the Lord is born to - day!

Slower

Let His love your souls a - dorn,— Christ the Lord is born!

Slower

Alleluia! Hearts to Heaven and Voices Raise

87 87. D.

CHRISTOPHER WORDSWORTH, 1807–1885

EDUARDO MARZO, 1852–1929

1. Al - le - lu - ia! Al - le - lu - ia! Hearts to heav'n and voic - es raise;
2. Now the i - ron bars are bro - ken, Christ from death to life is born.
3. Al - le - lu - ia! Al - le - lu - ia! Glo - ry be to God on high;

Sing to God a hymn of glad - ness, Sing to God a hymn of praise:
Glo - rious life, and life im - mor - tal, On this ho - ly Eas - ter morn:
Al - le - lu - ia to the Sav - ior Who has won the vic - to - ry;

He who on the cross as Sav - ior For the world's sal - va - tion bled,
Christ has tri - umphed, and we con - quer By His might - y en - ter - prise;
Al - le - lu - ia to the Spi - rit, Fount of love and sanc - ti - ty;

Je - sus Christ, the King of Glo - ry, Now is ris - en from the dead.
We with Him to life e - ter - nal By His res - ur - rec - tion rise.
Al - le - lu - ia! Al - le - lu - ia! To the Tri - une Maj - es - ty.

Nearer, My God, to Thee

BETHANY 64 64. 66 64

SARAH F. ADAMS, 1805–1848

LOWELL MASON, 1792–1872

1. Near - er, my God, to Thee, Near - er to Thee!
2. Though like the wan - der - er, The sun gone down,
3. There let the way ap - pear, Steps un - to heav'n;
4. Then, with my wak - ing thoughts Bright with Thy praise,
5. Or if, on joy - ful wing Cleav - ing the sky,

E'en though it be a cross That rais - eth me;
Dark - ness be o - ver me, My rest a stone;
All that Thou send - est me, In mer - cy giv'n;
Out of my ston - y griefs Beth - el I'll raise;
Sun, moon, and stars for - got, Up - ward I fly,

Still all my song shall be,
Yet in my dreams I'd be
An - gels to beck - on me Near - er, my God, to Thee,
So by my woes to be
Still all my song shall be,

Near - er, my God, to Thee, Near - er to Thee!

58

Rejoice, Ye Pure in Heart

MARION S. M., with Refrain

EDWARD H. PLUMPTRE, 1821–1891   ARTHUR H. MESSITER, 1831–1916

1. Re - joice, ye pure in heart, Re - joice, give thanks and sing;
2. Bright youth and snow-crowned age, Strong men and maid-ens fair,
3. Yes, on through life's long path, Still chant - ing as ye go;
4. Still lift your stan - dard high, Still march in firm ar - ray,

Your glo - rious ban - ner wave on high, The cross of Christ your King.
Raise high your free, ex - ult - ing song, God's won - drous praise de - clare.
From youth to age, by night and day, In glad - ness and in woe.
As war - riors thro' the dark - ness toil Till dawn the gold - en day.

Re - joice, re - joice, Re - joice, give thanks and sing.
Re - joice, re - joice,

Abide with Me, 'Tis Eventide

WELCOME GUEST   86 86. 86, with Refrain

MARTIN LOWRIE HOFFORD, 1825–1888

HARRISON MILLARD, 1830–1895

1. A - bide with me, 'tis e - ven - tide! The day is past and gone;
2. A - bide with me, 'tis e - ven - tide! Thy walk to - day with me
3. A - bide with me, 'tis e - ven - tide! And lone will be the night,

The shad - ows of the eve - ning fall, The night is com - ing on!
Has made my heart with - in me burn, As I com - muned with Thee.
If I can - not com - mune with Thee, Nor find in Thee my light.

With - in my heart a wel - come guest, With - in my home a - bide;
Thy ear - nest words have filled my soul And kept me near Thy side,
The dark - ness of the world I fear, Would in my home a - bide;

Oh, Sav - iour! stay this night with me, Be - hold 'tis e - ven - tide.

Oh, Sav - iour! stay this night with me, Be - hold 'tis e - ven - tide.

To Lowell Mason, Esq.

60   Once More, Before We Part

JESUS, THE SINNER'S FRIEND   66 66, with Refrain

ANONYMOUS   GEORGE WASHBOURN MORGAN, 1823–1892

1. Once more, be - fore we part, Bless the Re - deem - er's name;
2. Lord, in Thy grace we came; That bless - ing still im - part;
3. Still on Thy ho - ly Word We'd live, and feel, and grow;
4. Here, Lord, we came to live, And in Thy truth in - crease;
5. Now, Lord, be - fore we part, Help us to bless Thy name;

Let ev - 'ry tongue and heart Praise and a - dore the Lamb.
We met in Je - sus's name; In Je - sus's Name we part.
Go on to know the Lord, And prac - tice what we know.
All that's a - miss for - give, And send us home in peace.
May ev - 'ry tongue and heart Praise and a - dore the same.

Je - sus, the sin - ner's friend, Whom heav'n and Earth a - dore;

cresc.   **Ritard.**

Whose prais - es have no end— Praise Him for - ev - er - more.

Hail! Thou Long-Expected Jesus

87 87. D.

CHARLES WESLEY, 1707–1788

GEORGE WASHBOURN MORGAN, 1823–1892

1. Hail! thou long-ex-pect-ed Je-sus, Born to set Thy peo-ple free;
2. Born Thy peo-ple to de-liv-er, Born a child and yet a King.

From our sins and fears re-lease us, Let us find our rest in Thee.
Born to reign in us for-ev-er, Now Thy gra-cious king-dom bring.

Is-rael's strength and con-so-la-tion, Hope of all the saints, thou art;
By Thine own e-ter-nal Spir-it Rule in all our hearts a-lone;

Long de-sired of ev-'ry na-tion, Joy of ev-'ry wait-ing heart.
By Thine all-suf-fi-cient mer-it, Raise us to Thy glo-rious throne.

62 Inspirer and Hearer of Prayer

PLATT 88 88. D.

AUGUSTUS M. TOPLADY, 1740–1778

GEORGE WASHBOURN MORGAN, 1823–1892

1. In - spir - er and Hear - er of prayer, Thou Shep - herd and Guard -ian of Thine,
2. Thy min - is-t'ring spi - rits des - cend To watch while Thy saints are a - sleep;
3. Their wor-ship no in - ter - val knows; Their fer - vor is still on the wing;

My all to Thy cov - en - ant care I sleep -ing or wak - ing re - sign:
By day and by night they at - tend, The heirs of sal - va - tion to keep:
And, while they pro - tect my re - pose, They chant to the praise of my King.

If Thou are my Shield and my Sun, The night is no dark-ness to me;
Bright ser - aphs, des - patched from the throne, Re - pair to their sta - tions as-signed;
I, too, at the sea - son or - dained, Their chor - us for - ev - er shall join,

And fast as my min - utes roll on, They bring me but near - er to Thee.
And an - gels e - lect are sent down, To guard the re - deemed of man - kind.
And love and a - dore with-out end Their faith - ful Cre - a - tor and mine.

Still Thy Sorrow, Magdalena!

63

MAGDALENA   87 87. 87, with Alleluia

Ancient Latin hymn,
Tr. EDWARD ABIEL WASHBURN, 1819–1881

JOSEPH MOSENTHAL, 1834–1896

1. Still thy sor-row, Mag-da-le-na! Wipe the tear-drops from thine eyes;
2. Laugh with rap-ture, Mag-da-le-na! Be thy droop-ing fore-head bright;
3. Joy, ex-ult, O Mag-da-le-na! Christ from death the world has freed;
4. Lift thine eyes, O Mag-da-le-na! See! thy liv-ing Mas-ter stands;
5. Live, now live, O Mag-da-le-na! Shin-ing is thy new-born day;

Not at Si-mon's board thou kneel-est, Pour-ing thy re-pent-ant sighs;
Ban-ished now is ev-'ry an-guish, Breaks a-new thy morn-ing light;
End-ed are the days of dark-ness; He is ris'n, is ris'n in-deed.
See His face as ev-er smil-ing, See those wounds up-on His hands,
Lift thy heart in swell-ing mu-sic, Death's poor ter-ror flies a-way;

All with thy glad heart re-joi-ces, All things sing with hap-py voic-es—
Christ hath burst the rock-y pris-on, Con-quer-er of death a-ris-en;
Mourn no more the Lord de-part-ed, Run to wel-come Him glad-heart-ed,
O'er His feet, His side once bleed-ing, Now as pearls of light ex-ceed-ing,
Far from thee the tears of sad-ness, Wel-come love, and wel-come glad-ness!

Al - le - lu - ia, Al - le - lu - ia.

77

64   O Thou Whose Boundless Love Bestows

PRINCETON 88 88. 88 8. 10

HENRY VAN DYKE. 1852–1933

HORACE WADHAM NICHOLL, 1848–1922

1. O Thou whose bound-less love be-stows The joy of life, the hope of heav'n; Thou whose un-chart-ered mer-cy flows O'er all the bless-ings Thou hast giv'n; Thou, by whose light a-

2. Be Thou our strength when war's wild gust Ra-ges a-round us, loud and fierce; Con-firm our souls and let our trust Be like a wall that none can pierce; Give us the cour-age

3. O God, make us what Thou wilt; Guide Thou the la-bor of our hand; Let all our work be sure-ly built As Thou, the arch-i-tect, hast planned; But what-so-e'er Thy

65   In the Little Village of Bethlehem

THE BIRTHDAY OF A KING   10 6. 10 6, with Refrain

WILLIAM NEIDLINGER 1863–1924   WILLIAM NEIDLINGER 1863–1924

1. In the lit-tle vil-lage of Beth-le-hem, There lay a Child one day.
2. 'Twas a hum-ble birth-place, but oh, how much God gave to us that day;

And the sky was bright with a ho-ly light O'er the place where Je-sus lay.
From the man-ger bed what a path has led, What a per-fect, ho-ly way.

Al-le-lu-ia! Oh, how the an-gels sang. Al-le-lu-ia! How it rang!

And the sky was bright with a ho-ly light, 'Twas the birth-day of a King.

Come, Labor On

ORA LABORA 4. 10 10. 10 4

JANE LAURIE BORTHWICK, 1813–1897

T. TERTIUS NOBLE, 1867–1953

1. Come, la-bor on. Who dares stand i - dle on the har - vest plain,
2. Come, la-bor on. The en - e - my is watch-ing night and day,
3. Come, la-bor on. A - way with gloom - y doubts and faith-less fear!
4. Come, la-bor on. Claim the high call - ing an - gels can - not share—
5. Come, la-bor on. No time for rest, till glows the west-ern sky,

While all a - round him waves the gold - en grain? And to each ser - vant
To sow the tares, to snatch the seed a - way; While we in sleep our
No arm so weak but may do ser - vice here: By fee - blest a - gents
To young and old the gos - pel glad - ness bear; Re - deem the time; its
Till the long sha - dows o'er our path - way lie, And a glad sound comes

does the Mas - ter say, "Go work to - day."
du - ty have for - got, He slum - - ber'd not.
may our God ful - fil His right - - eous will.
hours too swift - ly fly. The night - - draws nigh.
with the set - ting sun,___ "Ser - - vants, well done."

Lift the Strain of High Thanksgiving

ALBANY 87 87. D.

JOHN ELLERTON, 1826–1893   GEORGE EDGAR OLIVER, 1856–1941

1. Lift the strain of high thanks-giv-ing! Tread with songs the hal-low'd way!
2. When the years had wrought their chang-es, He, our own un-chang-ing God,
3. En-ter then Thy gates with prais-es, Lord, be ours Thine Is-rael's prayer:
4. Fill this lat-ter house with glo-ry Great-er than the form-er knew;
5. Praise to Thee, Al-might-y Fa-ther, Praise to Thee, E-ter-nal Son,

Praise our fa-thers' God, for mer-cies, New to us their sons to-day:
Thought on this His ha-bi-tat-ion, Looked on His de-cayed a-bode;
"Rise in-to Thy place of rest-ing, Show Thy prom-ised pres-ence there!"
Clothe with right-eous-ness its priest-hood, Guide us all to rev-'rence true;
Praise to Thee, all-quick-'ning Spir-it, Ev-er bless-ed Three in One:

Here they built for Him a dwell-ing, Served Him here in a-ges past,
Heard our prayers, and helped our coun-sels, Blessed the sil-ver and the gold,
Let the grac-ious word be spok-en Here, as once on Si-on's height,
Let Thy Ho-ly One's an-oint-ing Here its sev'n-fold bless-ing shed;
Three-fold Pow'r and Grace and Wis-dom, Mold-ing out of sin-ful clay,

Fix'd it for His sure poss-ess-ion, Ho-ly ground, while time shall last.
Till once more His house is stand-ing Firm and state-ly as of old.
"This shall be My rest for ev-er, This my dwell-ing of de-light."
Spread for us the heav-'nly ban-quet, Sat-is-fy Thy poor with bread.
Liv-ing stones for that true tem-ple Which shall nev-er know de-cay.

Land Whose Olden Anthems Praise

AMERICA 66 88. 86

68

FREDERICK H. MARTENS, 1874–1932

LEO ORNSTEIN, 1895–2002

1. Land whose old-en an-thems praise What old tra-di-tion
2. We love thy glo-ry's bat-tle scars, The le-gends of thy
3. Thou, A-mer-i-ca, en-shrined In ev-'ry pa-triot

blessed, A-mer-i-ca, to thee we raise A
youth; And no less dear thy flag of stars, Yet
soul, To old-en greeds and ha-treds blind, In

song of these, the fair-er days When no-bler faith of
now a hope no sha-dow mars Has cast down the
un-it-y thy strength shall bind The man-y na-tions

man-kind lays the ghosts of hate to rest.
last world bars to friend-ship, peace and truth.
till they find In bro-ther-hood their goal.

83

Ancient of Days

ANCIENT OF DAYS 11 10. 11 10

WILLIAM C. DOANE, 1832–1913

HORATIO W. PARKER, 1856–1919

mf 1. An - cient of Days, Who sit - test, thron'd in glo - ry;
2. O Ho - ly Fa - ther, who hast led Thy chil - dren
3. O Ho - ly Je - sus, Prince of Peace and Sav - iour,
4. O Ho - ly Ghost, the Lord and the Life - giv - er,
5. O Tri - une God, with heart and voice a - dor - ing,

To Thee all knees are bent, all voi - ces pray;___
In all the a - ges, with the fire and cloud,___
To Thee we owe the peace that still pre - vails,___
Thine is the quick - 'ning pow'r that gives in - crease;___
Praise we the good - ness that doth crown our days;___

Thy love has blest the wide world's won - drous sto - ry,
Through seas dry - shod, through wea - ry wastes be - wil - d'ring;
Still - ing the rude wills of men's wild be - hav - ior,
From Thee have flowed, as from a pleas - ant riv - er,
Pray we that Thou wilt hear us, still im - plor - ing

With light and life since E - den's dawn - ing day.
To Thee, in rev - 'rent love, our hearts are bowd.
And calm - ing pas - sion's fierce and storm - y gales.
Our plen - ty, wealth, pros - per - i - ty, and peace.
Thy love and fa - vor kept to us al - ways.

There's a Church in the Valley by the Wildwood

THE CHURCH IN THE WILDWOOD 76 76, with Refrain

WILLIAM S. PITTS, 1830–1918

WILLIAM S. PITTS, 1830–1918

70

71   Lord of the Nations and God of All People

HOLY TRINITY   10 10. 10 10

CUTHBERT PRATT, 1916–1979   BRONSON RAGAN, 1915–1971

1. Lord of the na - tions and God of all peo - ple,
2. Add to our prayers the zeal of en - deav - or,
3. Grant we my hon - or our found - ers and fore - bears,
4. So shall we off - er in lives, more than lan - guage,

Quick - en the praise which we off - fer to Thee.
Fill all our gifts with the off - er - ing of self.
Not in re - flec - tion or mem - o - ry a - lone,
Praise to the Fa - ther and praise to the Son,

Strength - en the ties that bind us to - get - her,
Help us to hear that in learn - ing we pro - fit,
But in that strength that true wor - ship off - ers,
Lives Spi - rit guid - ed, our God tru - ly hon - ored,

Help us to serve and Thy pur - pose to see.
Not our own way, but Thy plan for our health.
Spread - ing Thy Gos - pel to make us Thine own.
Our course com - plete and His vic - to - ry won.

Praise, My Soul, the King of Heaven

THURMAN 87 87. 87

HENRY FRANCIS LYTE, 1794–1847

McNEIL ROBINSON, 1943–2015

1. Praise my soul, the King of heav - en; to His feet thy tri - bute bring.
2. Praise Him for His grace and fa - vor to our fath - ers in dis - tress;
3. Fa - ther - like, He tends and spares us; Well our fee - ble frame He knows;
4. An - gels in the height, a - dore Him; Ye be - hold Him face to face;

Ran - somed, healed, re - stored, for - giv - en, ev - er - more His prais - es sing.
Praise Him, still the same as ev - er, slow to chide, and swift to bless;
In His hands He gen - tly bears us, Res - cues us from all our foes;
Saints tri - um - phant, bow be - fore Him; Gath ered in from ev - 'ry race.

Al - le - lu - ia! Al - le - lu - ia! Praise the ev - er - last - ing King!
Al - le - lu - ia! Al - le - lu - ia! Glo - rious in His faith - ful - ness.
Al - le - lu - ia! Al - le - lu - ia! Wide - ly yet His mer - cy flows.
Al - le - lu - ia! Al - le - lu - ia! Praise with us the God of grace.

73   Welcome, Happy Morning!

65 65. D, with Refrain

VENANTIUS FORTUNATUS, c. 530–609
Tr. JOHN ELLERTON, 1826–1893

CHARLES B. RUTENBER, 1849–1918

CHORUS

89

74   **O Merciful One**

LINCOLN 5 10. 10 6

ELIZABETH LLOYD HOWELL, 1811–1896   SUMNER SALTER, 1856–1944

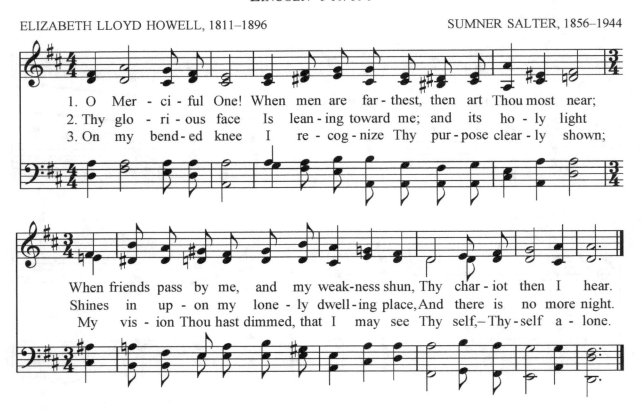

1. O Mer - ci - ful One! When men are far - thest, then art Thou most near;
2. Thy glo - ri - ous face Is lean - ing toward me; and its ho - ly light
3. On my bend - ed knee I re - cog - nize Thy pur - pose clear - ly shown;

When friends pass by me, and my weak-ness shun, Thy char - iot then I hear.
Shines in up - on my lone - ly dwell - ing place, And there is no more night.
My vis - ion Thou hast dimmed, that I may see Thy self,–Thy - self a - lone.

75   **His Are the Thousand Sparkling Rills**

BEDFORD 88 86.

CECIL FRANCES ALEXANDER, 1818–1895   ROLLIN SMITH, b. 1942

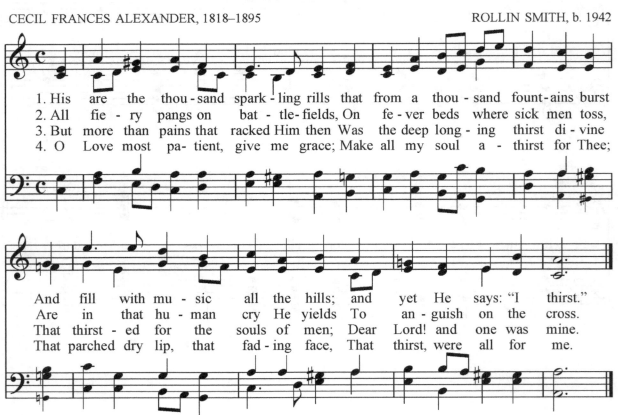

1. His are the thou - sand spark - ling rills that from a thou - sand fount - ains burst
2. All fie - ry pangs on bat - tle-fields, On fe - ver beds where sick men toss,
3. But more than pains that racked Him then Was the deep long - ing thirst di - vine
4. O Love most pa - tient, give me grace; Make all my soul a - thirst for Thee;

And fill with mu - sic all the hills; and yet He says: "I thirst."
Are in that hu - man cry He yields To an - guish on the cross.
That thirst - ed for the souls of men; Dear Lord! and one was mine.
That parched dry lip, that fad - ing face, That thirst, were all for me.

My Days Are Gliding Swiftly By

SHINING SHORE   87 87, with Refrain

DAVID NELSON, 1793–1844

GEORGE F. ROOT, 1820–1895

1. My days are glid-ing swift-ly by, And I, a pil-grim stran-ger,
2. Our ab-sent King the watch-word gave: "Let ev-'ry lamp be burn-ing";
3. Should com-ing days be dark and cold. We will not yield to sor-row;
4. Let sor-row's rud-est tem-pest blow. Each cord on earth to sev-er;

Would not de-tain them as they fly, Those hours of toil and dan-ger.
We look a-far a-cross the wave, Our dis-tant home dis-cern-ing.
For hope will sing, with cour-age bold. There's glo-ry on the mor-row.
Our King says, Come, and there's our home For-ev-er! O for-ev-er!

For, O we stand on Jor-dan's strand, Our friends are pass-ing o-ver;

And just be-fore, the Shin-ing Shore We may al-most dis-cov-er.

77

Hark! Hark, My Soul

11 10. 11 10, with Refrain

FREDERICK W. FABER, 1814–1863

HARRY ROWE SHELLEY, 1858–1947

1. Hark! hark, my soul! An - gel - ic songs are swell - ing
2. On - ward we go, for still we hear them sing - ing,
3. Far, far a - way, like bells at eve - ning peal - ing,

O'er earth's green fields and o - cean's wave - beat shore;
"Come, wear - y soul, for Je - sus bids you come";
The voice of Je - sus sounds o'er land and sea,

How sweet the truth those bless - ed strains are tell - ing
And through the dark, its ech - oes sweet - ly ring - ing,
And la - den souls by thou - sands meek - ly steal - ing,

Of that new life when sin shall be_____ no more!
The mu - sic of the Gos - pel leads_____ us home.
Kind Shep - herd, turn their wea - ry steps_____ to Thee.

92

4. Rest comes at length, though life be long and dreary;
   The day must dawn, and darksome night be past;
All journeys end in welcome to the weary,
   And heaven, the heart's true home, will come at last.

5. Angels, sing on! your faithful watches keeping;
   Sing us sweet fragments of the songs above;
Till morning's joy shall end the night of weeping,
   And life's long shadows break in cloudless love.

78 People of Earth

NATIONS, ADORE!   10 10. 10 10, with Refrain

HARRY ROWE SHELLEY, 1858–1947   HARRY ROWE SHELLEY, 1858–1947

Marcato

1. Peo - ple of earth, Bowed with weight of sad - ness, Up - ward your
2. Far in the east, Told in song and sto - ry Je - sus, our

hearts raise and List to the strain Cease from your toil,
Sa - viour, was Born on this day, Low - ly on earth,

Lift your pray'rs with glad - ness; Gone is your sor - row; now
Now He reigns in glo - ry; Hark to His teach - ings, give

Join the re - frain: Na - tions: Come and a - dore! Wor - ship the King!
ear and o - bey!

Lord, Lord of Thy won - drous Love Our praise we sing. praise we sing.

What Beauteous Sun-Surpassing Star

QUÆ STELLA SOLE PULCHRIOR 87 87. D.

CHARLES COFFIN, 1676–1749

CARL G. SCHMIDT, 1868–1938

1. What beau - teous sun - sur - pass - ing star, O'er Beth - l'hem's lone - ly road,
2. While thus the star its light im - parts, A ray with - in doth shine,
3. O Je - sus, morn - ing star, our hearts Cleanse with Thy light with - in,

Re - veals a ris - ing bright - er far, And shows the cra - dled God!
Which leads a few but faith - ful hearts To seek the glor - 'ious sign.
And suf - fer not the tempt - er's arts To lure us back to sin.

The star from Ja - cob see a - rise, By proph - ets long fore - told;
No dan - gers can their pur - pose shake; Love suf - fers no de - lay.
The light of Gen - tile lands a - dore, The Day - spring from on high;

The si - lent night - ly mes - sen - ger, The na - tions East be - hold.
Home, kin - dred, coun - try, they for - sake; God calls, and they o - bey.
A - like the Fa - ther ev - er - more, And spir - it mag - ni - fy.

Hymn for Healing

LAFAYETTE 87 87. 87

EDWARD J. MORAN

HAMPSON A. SISLER, b. 1932

1. Christ our Health and Christ our heal - ing, Hear our
2. Yea, though pain and plague af - flict us, Death sur -
3. Take our bod - ies, bruised and bro - ken, Break them
4. Speak of Love that dares be name - less, Love that

bro - thers', sis - ters' plea. Firm us up in faith and
round us like a shroud, Christ, and Christ a - lone in -
as Thy liv - ing bread. Make of pas - sion wounds a
calls us to this place. Nor shall fe - ver still in -

feel - ing, Set our bod - ies, spir - its free. Lus - ter
fect us 'Til our lives be Christ en - dowed. From our
to - ken Cleansed and filled with wine in - stead. In this
flame us Save the ar - dor of Thy grace. Christ, Thy

to all flesh re - veal - ing, Christ our sure im - mun - i - ty.
fears now re - sur - rect us, Lead us forth in fire and cloud.
sac - ra - ment be spo - ken Words of sol - ace still un - said.
paths are pure and blame - less Peace at - tend us all our days.

5. Christ for now and Christ for ages,
   Christ who lives in plague and pain.
   Christ upon a cross courageous
   Christ who died shall ever reign.
   Christ alive and Christ contageous
   Christ, Omega, come again.

6. Christ our Health and Christ our healing,
   Christ our struggle yet to be.
   Christ our Font of Faith and feeling,
   Christ our final victory.
   Christ our Love, to life appealing,
   Christ our sure immunity.

We May Not Climb the Heavenly Steeps   81

86 86

JOHN GREENLEAF WHITTIER, 1807–1892   KATE S. CHITTENDEN, 1856–1949

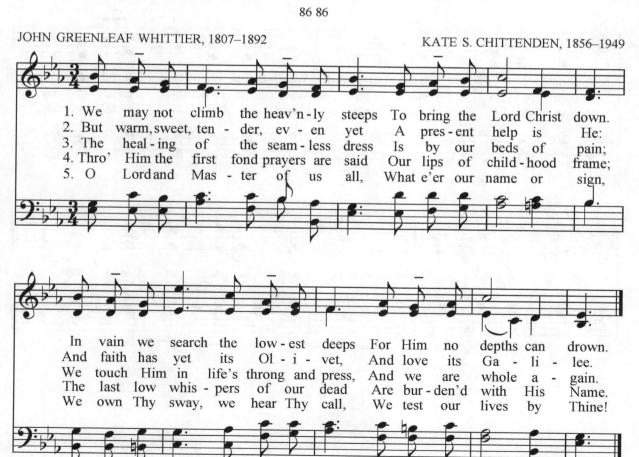

1. We may not climb the heav'n - ly steeps To bring the Lord Christ down.
2. But warm, sweet, ten - der, ev - en yet A pres - ent help is He:
3. The heal - ing of the seam - less dress Is by our beds of pain;
4. Thro' Him the first fond prayers are said Our lips of child - hood frame;
5. O Lord and Mas - ter of us all, What e'er our name or sign,

In vain we search the low - est deeps For Him no depths can drown.
And faith has yet its Ol - i - vet, And love its Ga - li - lee.
We touch Him in life's throng and press, And we are whole a - gain.
The last low whis - pers of our dead Are bur - den'd with His Name.
We own Thy sway, we hear Thy call, We test our lives by Thine!

82 Once a Little Baby Lay

77 66. 77 66

EMILIE POULSSON, 1853–1939

GERRIT SMITH, 1859–1912

1. Once a lit - tle ba - by lay, Cra - dled on the fra - grant hay,
2. By the shin - ing vi - sion taught, Shep - herds for the Christ Child sought,
3. And to - day the whole glad earth Prai - ses God for that child's birth,

Long a - go on Christ - mas, Long a - go on Christ - mas;

Org. Ped.

Strang - er bed a babe n'er found, Won - d'ring cat - tle stood a - round,
Guid - ed in a star - lit way, Wise men came their gifts to pay,
For the Life, the Truth, the Way, Came to bless the earth that day,

Ped.

Long a - go on Christ - mas, Long a - go on Christ - mas.

God Who Madest Earth and Heaven

EVENING PRAYER 84 84. 88 84

REGINALD HEBER, 1783–1826

FANNY MORRIS SPENCER, 1867–1932+

1. God, Who mad-est earth and heav-en, Dark - ness and light;
2. And when morn a - gain shall call us To run life's way
3. Guard us wak-ing, guard us sleep-ing, And when we die,

Who the day for toil hast giv-en, For rest the night;
May we still what-e'er be-fall us Thy will o - bey.
May we in Thy might-y keep-ing all peace-ful lie;

May Thine An - gel guards de-fend us, Slum-ber sweet Thy mer-cy send us;
From the pow'r of ev - il hide us, In the nar-row path-way guide us,
When the last dread call shall wake us, Do not Thou, our God for-sake us,

Ho - ly dreams and hopes at-tend us, This live-long night.
Nor Thy smile be e'er de - nied us The live-long day.
But to reign in glo-ry take us With Thee on high.

The Sun Is Sinking Fast

64 66. 64 66

Latin, 18th cent.
Tr. EDWARD CASWALL, 1814–1878

FANNY MORRIS SPENCER, 1867–1932+

1. The sun is sink-ing fast, The day - light dies;
2. So now her-self my soul Would whol - ly give
3. Save that His Will be done, What - e'er be - tide,

Let love a-wake, and pay Her ev'n - ing sac - ri - fice.
In - to His sa - cred charge In whom all spi - rits live;
Dead to her - self, and dead In Him to all be - side.

As Christ up - on the Cross, His Head in - clined,
So now be - neath His eye Would calm - ly rest,
Thus would I live; yet now Not I, but He

And to His Fa - ther's hands His part - ing Soul re - signed.
With - out a wish or thought A - bid - ing in the breast.
In all His pow'r and love Hence - forth a - live in me.

Jesus, Thou Source of Calm Repose

DARTMOUTH L. M.

CHARLES WESLEY, 1707–1788

MAX SPICKER, 1858–1912

1. Je - sus, Thou source of calm re - pose, All full - ness dwells in
2. Je - sus, our Com - fort - er Thou art; Our rest in toil, our
3. In want, our plen - ti - ful sup - ply; In weak - ness, our al -

Thee di - vine; Our strength to quell the proud - est foes;
ease in pain; The balm to heal each brok - en heart,
might - y pow'r; In bonds, our per - fect li - ber - ty;

Our light, in deep - est gloom to shine; Thou art our fort - ress,
In storms our peace, in loss our gain; Our joy be -neath the
Our re - fuge, in temp - ta - tion's hour. Our com - fort when in

Largo

strength and tow'r, Our trust and por - tion, ev - er - more.
world - ling's frown; In shame, our glo - ry and our crown.
grief and thrall; Our life in death; our all in all. A - men.

Hark! Hark! The Organ Loudly Peals

An Organ Hymn   87 87. 66 66. 7

GODFREY THRING, 1823–1903

FREDERICK SWANN, b. 1931

♩ = 96–104

Hark! hark! the or-gan loud-ly peals, Our thank-ful hearts in - vit - ing

1. To sing our great Cre - a - tor's praise,
2. To sing the praise of Christ our King,
3. To sing the Ho - ly Spi - rit's praise,
4. To high up - raise our songs of praise,

Both rich and poor u - nit - ing!

Ye heav'ns and earth re - joice!_____ And ev - 'ry
Who left His throne on high,_____ And low - ly
Who bids us flee from sin,_____ And makes us
To God the Fath - er, Son,_____ And Spir - it,

heart and voice Your joy - ous strains up - raise In notes of
came to die, That we from earth might rise To realms be-
pure with - in, Till, warmed with heav'n - ly love We yearn to
Three in One. Till, soar - ing higher and higher We join the

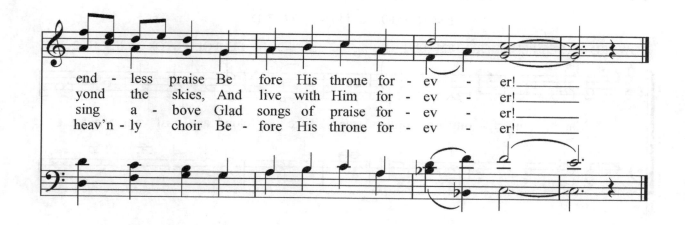

end - less praise Be fore His throne for - ev - er!_____
yond the skies, And live with Him for - ev - er!_____
sing a - bove Glad songs of praise for - ev - er!_____
heav'n - ly choir Be - fore His throne for - ev - er!_____

Break Thou the Bread of Life

87

BREAD OF LIFE 64 64. D.

MARY ARTEMISIA LATHBURY, 1841–1913

WILLIAM F. SHERWIN, 1826–1888

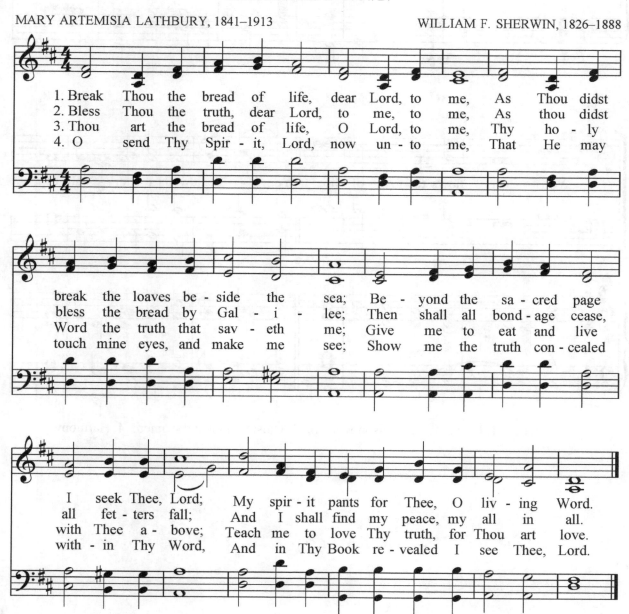

1. Break Thou the bread of life, dear Lord, to me, As Thou didst
2. Bless Thou the truth, dear Lord, to me, to me, As thou didst
3. Thou art the bread of life, O Lord, to me, Thy ho - ly
4. O send Thy Spir - it, Lord, now un - to me, That He may

break the loaves be - side the sea; Be - yond the sa - cred page
bless the bread by Gal - i - lee; Then shall all bond - age cease,
Word the truth that sav - eth me; Give me to eat and live
touch mine eyes, and make me see; Show me the truth con - cealed

I seek Thee, Lord; My spir - it pants for Thee, O liv - ing Word.
all fet - ters fall; And I shall find my peace, my all in all.
with Thee a - bove; Teach me to love Thy truth, for Thou art love.
with - in Thy Word, And in Thy Book re - vealed I see Thee, Lord.

103

88 March, March Onward, Soldiers True

PROCESSIONAL HYMN 77 77. D.

EDWARD HAYES PLUMPTRE, 1821–1891   LEOPOLD STOKOVSKI, 1882–1977

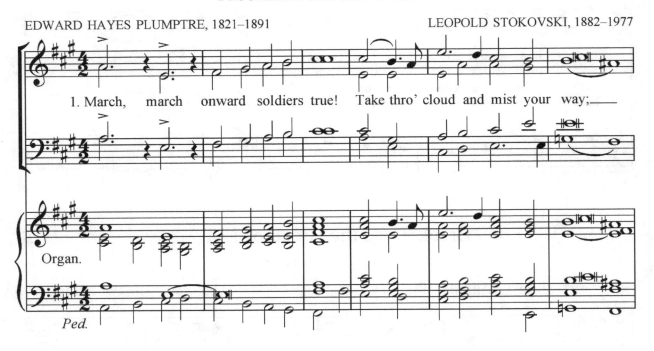

1. March, march onward soldiers true! Take thro' cloud and mist your way;___

Organ.

Ped.

Yon - der flows the fount of life, Yon - der dwells e - ter - nal day.

Stanzas 1. Harmony; 2. Unison women; 3. Unison: men and women; 4. Harmony

March, tho' myr-iad foes are nigh, For-ward, till ye reach the shore:

Then, when all the strife is done, Rest in peace for ev-er-more.

II.
Hark, hark, loud the trumpet sounds!
  Wake, ye children of the light;
Time is past for sloth and sleep,
  Wake, and arm you for the fight.
Spear and sword each warrior needs;
  Foes are round you, friends are few;
Faint not, though the way be long;
  Fainting, still your way pursue.

III.
See, see, yonder shines your home—
  Gates of pearl and walls of gold,
Joy that heart hath never known,
  Bliss that tongue hath never told!
Victors then thro' Christ your Lord,
  Gathered round His glorious throne,
Be it yours to sing His praise,
  Praise that He, your King, shall own.

IV.
Praise, praise Him who reigns on high!
  Praise the co-eternal Son!
Praise the Spirit, Lord of Life!
  Praise the blessed Three in One!
Praise Him, ye who toil and fight!
  Praise Him, ye who bear the palm!
As the sound of mighty seas
  Pour your everlasting psalm!   AMEN.

To Captain J.R. De Lamar

To Our Country Rich in Deeds

OUR COUNTRY 78 84, with Refrain

FRANK TAFT, 1861–1947   FRANK TAFT, 1861–1947

1. To our coun-try rich in deeds, We pledge our lives her name to save;
2. When the call to arms re-sounds, In home and flag our pride in-crease;
3. Guid-ed by His just de-crees, We'll tri-umph o-ver ev-'ry foe.

Her sa-cred ban-ner long shall wave O'er land and sea.
The Lord of Hosts, the King of Peace, Our strength in-spires.
All hon-or now, as long a-go, To this fair name!

REFRAIN (*with vigor and decision*)

Hail! all hail, A-mer-i-ca! Land of free-dom, truth, and light;

We sing thy praise, we know thy might; De-moc-ra-cy for-ev-er!

I Have a Glorious Hope!

90

86 86. 66 66

AUGUSTA BROWNE GARRETT, 1820–1882   AUGUSTA BROWNE GARRETT, 1820–1882

1. "I have a glo rious, glo - rious hope!" a hope which brigh-ter glows,
2. "I have a glo rious, glo - rious hope!" when spheres are all a - flame,
3. "I have a glo rious, glo - rious hope!" no Day of Wrath for me,
4. "I have a glo rious, glo - rious hope!" the Ci - ty is in sight,
5. "I have a glo rious, glo - rious hope!" Lord, for Thy Son's dear sake,

As near my steps that sol - emn tide, whose depths no mor - tal knows;
Se - rene in Him I safe - ly trust, I tri - umph in His name.
For me the great Arch - an - gel's trump will be sweet mel - o - dy;
With throngs of hap - py prais - ing saints all robed in lus - trous white,
In - to Thy heav'nly gar - ner pure Thy long - ing ser - vant take;

But nought to me its depths, its cur - rent fierce and wide,
Fare - well, brief world, fare - well, with all thy care and woe,
Fresh from its qui - et sleep my quick - en'd flesh shall soar,
And 'mid them fa - ces dear, long van - ished from the earth,
The Riv - er brink is reached, I hear the songs of home;

For on His arm I lean, on Christ the Cru - ci - fied.
The con - flict's past for aye, to end - less peace I go.
And clasp its spi - rit self - u - nit - ed ev - er - more.
Now smil - ing in the grace of the cel - les - tial birth.
Thou, loved in youth, in age, Sav - iour, to Thee I come!

107

91 Run through Glad Morning-Lustered Streets

DAY OF DAYS 88 88. 88

CAROL LOTT MONOHAN, 1922–1996

F. ANTHONY THURMAN, b. 1966

1. Run through glad morn-ing - lus-ter'd streets on feet that swift-ly
2. The Sab-bath done, two Mar-ys came with spi-ces to a-
3. At dawn, tri-um-phal, Christ a-rose. Pro-claim your joy, that

skim the clay. Let morn-ing wind un-tan-gle grief from
noint their Lord. He was not there! Two shin-ing ones re-
time is blest! Our God In-car-nate lives a-gain; since

hair un-bound in dis - a - ray. Let morn-ing shine a-way the night; dry
mind-ed them of Je-sus' word: "Tho' slain by those of gross in-tent, in
Ad-am's fall, this day is blest! E - ter - nal Love an-nounc-es Life; we

tears from sor-row's eye a - way!
three days I shall break Death's cord!"
are re-deemed, Death laid to rest!

For Randy and Donna Bremer

Away in a Manger

BREMER 11 11. 11 11

ANONYMOUS

F. ANTHONY THURMAN, b. 1966

1. A - way in a man - ger, no crib for his bed,
2. The cat - tle are low - ing, the poor ba - by wakes,
3. Be near me, Lord Je - sus; I ask thee to stay

The lit - tle Lord Je - sus laid down His sweet head.
But lit - tle Lord Je - sus, no cry - ing he makes.
Close by me for - ev - er and love me, I pray.

The stars in the sky looked down where he lay,
I love thee, Lord Je - sus, look down from the sky,
Bless all the dear chil - dren in thy ten - der care,

The lit - tle Lord Je - sus, a - sleep on the hay.
And stay by my side un - til morn - ing is nigh.
And fit us for heav - en to live with thee there.

Stanzas 1–2: *Little Children's Book for Schools and Families*, ca. 1885.
Stanza 3: *Gabriel's Vineyard Songs*, 1892.

92

93 Ride On! Ride On in Majesty

Lohengrin, Act 1, Scene 3   L. M.

HENRY HART MILMAN, 1791–1868

RICHARD WAGNER, 1813–1883
Arr. HOMER A. NORRIS, 1860–1920

1. Ride on! ride on in maj - es - ty! Hark! All the tribes Ho - san - na cry; O Sav - iour meek, pur - sue Thy road.
2. Ride on! ride on in maj - es - ty! In low - ly pomp ride on to die: O Christ, Thy tri - umphs now be - gin
3. Ride on! ride on in maj - es - ty! The wing - ed squad - rons of the sky Look down with sad and won - d'ring eyes
4. Ride on! ride on in maj - es - ty! Thy last and fierc - est strife is nigh. The Fa - ther on His glo - rious throne
5. Ride on! ride on in maj - es - ty! In low - ly pomp ride on to die, bow Thy meek head to mor - tal pain,

With palms and scat - ter'd gar - ments
O'er cap - tive death and con - quered
To see th'ap - proach - ing sac - ri -
Ex - pects His own a - noint - ed
Then take, O Christ, Thy powr and

Last verse.

strow'd.
sin.
fice.
Son.

reign. A - - - men.

He Dies! The Friend of Sinners dies!

1. He dies! the Friend of sinners dies!
   Lo! Salem's daughters weep around.
   A solemn darkness veils the skies;
   A sudden trembling shakes the ground.

2. Here's love and grief beyond degree:
   The Lord of glory dies for men;
   But lo, what sudden joys we see!
   Jesus, the dead, revives again.

3. The rising God forsakes the tomb!
   The tomb in vain forbids His rise:
   Cherubic legions guard Him home,
   And shout Him welcome to the skies.

4. Break off your tears, ye saints, and tell
   How high your great Deliv'rer reigns.
   Sing how He spoiled the hosts of hell,
   And led the monster, Death, in chains.

5. Say, "Live forever, wondrous King,
   Born to redeem, and strong to save!"
   Then ask the monster, "Where's thy sting?
   And where's thy vict'ry, boasting grave?"

ISAAC WATTS, 1674–1748

94

O Thou, Whose Own Vast Temple Stands

VOGRICH C. M.

WILLIAM CULLEN BRYANT, 1794–1878

MAX VOGRICH, 1852–1916

1. O Thou, whose own vast tem - ple stands, Built o - ver earth and sea,_____ Ac - cept the walls that hu - man hands Have raised to wor - ship Thee._____

2. Lord, from Thine in - most glo - ry send, With - in these walls t'a - bide,_____ The peace that dwell - eth with - out end, Se - rene - ly by Thy side!_____

3. May er - ring minds, that wor - ship here, Be taught the bet - ter way;_____ And they who mourn, and they who fear, Be strength - ened as they pray._____

4. May faith grow firm, and love grow warm, And pure de - vo - tion rise,_____ While, round these hal - lowed walls, the storm Of earth - born pas - sion dies._____ A - men.

The Harp at Nature's Advent Strung

95

TALLIS C. M.

JOHN GREENLEAF WHITTIER, 1807–1892

JULIAN WACHNER, b. 1969

1. The harp at na - ture's ad - vent strung Has nev - er ceased to play;
2. And prayer is made and prayer is giv'n By all things near and far;
3. The winds with hymns of praise are loud, Or low with sobs of pain,
4. The blue sky is the tem - ple's arch, Its tran - sept, earth and air,
5. So na - ture keeps the rev - 'rent frame With which her years be - gan,

The song the stars of morn - ing sung Has nev - er died a - way.
The o - cean look - eth up to heav'n And mir - rors ev - 'ry star.
The thun - der - or - gan of the cloud, The drop - ping tears of rain.
The mus - ic of its star - ry march The cho - rus of a prayer.
And all her signs and voic - es shame The pray'r - less heart of man.

Gentle Jesus, Meek and Mild

96

CHARLES WESLEY, 1707–1788

77 77

JOHN PAUL MORGAN, 1841–1879

1. Gen - tle Jes - us, meek and mild, Look up - on a lit - tle child;
2. Fain I would to Thee be brought; Grac - ious God for - bid it not;
3. O sup - ply my ev - ery want, Feed the young and ten - der plant.

Pit - y my sim - plic - i - ty Suf - fer me to come to Thee.
In the King - dom of Thy grace; Give a lit - tle child a place.
Day and night my Keep - er be, Ev - ery mo - ment watch round me.

97

Strife at Last Is Ended

PEACE 65 65

RODMAN WANAMAKER, 1863–1928   RODMAN WANAMAKER, 1863–1928

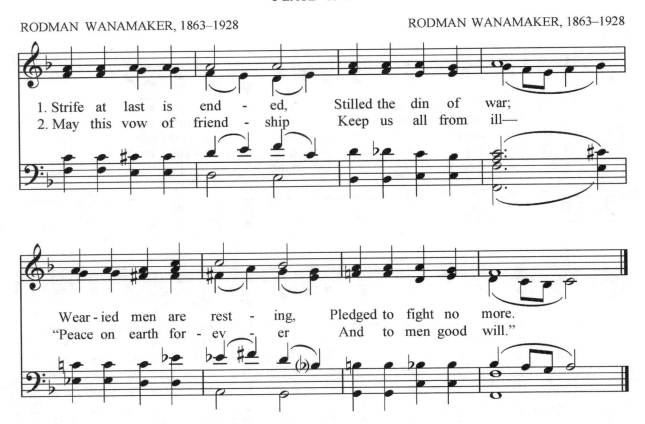

1. Strife at last is end - ed, Stilled the din of war;
2. May this vow of friend - ship Keep us all from ill—

Wear - ied men are rest - ing, Pledged to fight no more.
"Peace on earth for - ev - er And to men good will."

98

Bread of the World, in Mercy Broken

BETHSAIDA 98 98

REGINALD HEBER, 1783–1826   S. AUSTEN PEARCE, 1836–1900

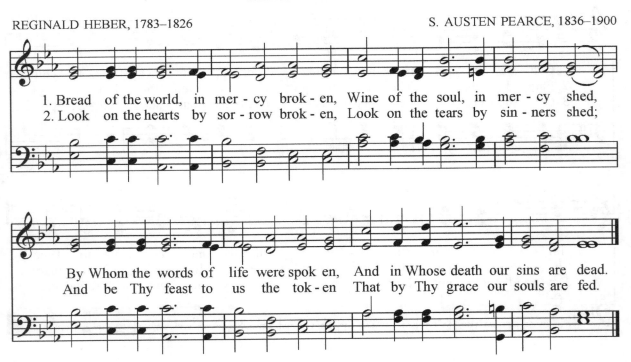

1. Bread of the world, in mer - cy brok - en, Wine of the soul, in mer - cy shed,
2. Look on the hearts by sor - row brok - en, Look on the tears by sin - ners shed;

By Whom the words of life were spok en, And in Whose death our sins are dead.
And be Thy feast to us the tok - en That by Thy grace our souls are fed.

God of Our Fathers, Whose Almighty Hand

NATIONAL HYMN 10 10. 10 10

DANIEL C. ROBERTS, 1841–1907

GEORGE WILLIAM WARREN, 1828–1902

Trumpets before each stanza

1. God of our fa - thers, whose al - migh - ty hand
2. Thy love di - vine hath led us in the past,
3. From war's a - larms, from dead - ly pes - ti - lence,
4. Re - fresh Thy peo - ple on their toil - some way,

Leads forth in beau - ty all the star - ry band
In this free land by Thee our lot is cast;
Be Thy strong arm our ev - er sure de - fense;
Lead us from night to nev - er - end - ing day;

Of shin - ing worlds in splen - dor through the skies,
Be Thou our rul - er, guard - ian, guide, and stay,
Thy true re - lig - ion in our hearts in - crease,
Fill all our lives with love and grace di - vine,

Our grate - ful songs be - fore Thy throne a - rise.
Thy Word our law, Thy paths our cho - sen way.
Thy boun - teous good - ness nour - ish us in peace.
And glo - ry, laud, and praise be ev - er Thine.

115

100 Our Glowing Praise to Thee

AMERICAN ANTHEM 66 66. 66 86

ANGELA MORGAN, ca. 1875–1957   DAVID McK. WILLIAMS, 1887–1978

1. Our glow-ing praise to thee, Thou gi - ant soul set free!
2. Thy soar-ing walls and spires, Thy rails and sing-ing wires
3. Thou shin-ing land and great, Ful - fill thy loft - ier fate;
4. Trans - fig - ured shalt thou stand, My loved ma - jes - tic land,
5. A - mer - i - ca, give heed! Thy no - bler quest - ing speed,

The lungs of At - las roar A - cross thy thresh - ing floor;
Be - come the might - y strings Where God His an - them rings,
Thou glo - ri - ous and wise Whose tow - ers touch the skies.
With vis - ions new - ly born Of earth's pri - me - val morn
Nor wealth nor pride a - lone shall bring thee to thine own.

The heart of Vul - can beats With - in thy ci - ty streets,
The thun - der of thy mills, The chant - ing of thy hills,
The loins of nat - ions pour Their child - ren at thy door.
When tree and star and sod Were mol - ten thoughts of God,
Re - lease thy soul at last In deeds of cour - age vast,

Jove's sin - ews in thy strength un - furled
Are yearn - ings of the u - ni - verse
That thou God's ma - gic word shalt find—
In cos - mic fur - na - ces at last
Nor pause till peace has come to birth

Co - los - sus of the world.
Ar - tic - u - late in thee.
The one - ness of man - kind.
His dreams of thee were cast.
And love en - folds the earth.

101   Brief Life Is Here Our Portion

LUDLOW 76 76. 76 76

BERNARD OF CLUNY, 12th century
JOHN MASON NEALE, 1818–1866

SAMUEL P. WARREN, 1841–1915

1. Brief life is here our por - tion; Brief sor - row, short-lived care;
2. And now we fight the bat - tle, But then shall wear the crown
3. The morn-ing shall a - wak - en, The shad-ows shall de - cay;

The life that knows no end - ing, The tear - less life, is there.
Of full and ev - er - last - ing And pas - sion-less re - nown.
And each true heart - ed serv - ant Shall shine as doth the day.

O hap - py ret - ri - bu - tion! Short toil, e - ter - nal rest;
But they who now in - struct us Shall then be seen and known;
There fa - ther, moth - er, chil - dren, Shall see each oth - er's face;

For mor - tals and for sin - ners A man - sion with the blest!
And they who know and see them Shall have them for their own.
And we be - hold for - ev - er A hap - py hu - man race.

O Little Town of Bethlehem

BETHLEHEM 86 86. 76 86

PHILLIPS BROOKS, 1835–1893

R. HUNTINGTON WOODMAN, 1861–1943

1. O lit-tle town of Beth-le-hem, How still we see thee lie!
2. For Christ is born of Ma-ry; And gath-ered all a-bove,
3. How si-lent-ly, how si-lent-ly, The won-drous Gift is giv'n!
4. Where child-ren pure and hap-py Pray to the bless-èd Child;

A-bove thy deep and dream-less sleep The si-lent stars go by.
While mor-tals sleep, the an-gels keep Their watch of won-d'ring love.
So God im-parts to hu-man hearts The bless-ings of His Heav'n.
Where mis-er-y cries out to Thee, Son of the Moth-er mild;

Yet in thy dark streets shin-eth The ev-er-last-ing Light!
O morn-ing stars, to-geth-er Pro-claim the ho-ly birth,
No ear may hear His com-ing, But in this world of sin,
Where Char-i-ty stands watch-ing, And Faith holds wide the door,—

The hopes and fears of all the years Are met in thee to-night.
And prais-es sing to God the King, And peace to all on earth!
Where meek souls will re-ceive Him still, The dear Christ en-ters in.
The dark night wakes, the glo-ry breaks, And Christ-mas comes once more.

103   **Only Begotten, Word of God Eternal**

ISTE CONFESSOR. 11 11. 11 5

Latin, ca. 9th century
Tr. MAXWELL J. BLACKER, 1822–1888

PIETRO A. YON, 1886–1943

Allegro mæstoso ♩ = 100

1. On - ly be - got - ten, Word of God e - ter - nal, Lord of cre-
2. This is Thy_ tem - ple; here Thy pres - ence - cham - ber; Here may Thy
3. Lord, we be - seech Thee, as we throng Thy tem - ple, By Thy past
4. God in three Per - sons, Fa - ther ev - er - last - ing, Son co - e -

a - tion, mer - ci - ful and migh - ty, Hear now Thy ser - vants,
ser - vants, at the mys - tic ban - quet, Hum - bly a - dor - ing,
bless - ings, by Thy pres - ent boun - ty, Fa - vor Thy chil - dren,
ter - nal, ev - er - bless - ed Spi - rit, Thine be the glo - ry,

when their joy - ful voic - es Rise to Thy pres - ence.
take Thy Bo - dy bro - ken, Drink of Thy chal - ice.
and with ten - der mer - cy Hear our pe - ti - tions.
praise, and a - do - ra - tion, Now and for - ev - er.

Love Divine, All Loves Excelling 104

BEECHER 87 87. D.

CHARLES WESLEY, 1707–1788 JOHN ZUNDEL, 1815–1882

1. Love di - vine, all loves ex - cel - ling, Joy of heav'n, to earth come down;
2. Breathe, O breathe Thy lov - ing Spir - it In - to ev - 'ry trou - bled breast!
3. Come, Al - might - y to de - liv - er, Let us all Thy grace re - ceive;
4. Fin - ish, then, Thy new cre - a - tion; Pure and spot - less let us be;
Fix in us Thy hum - ble dwell - ing; All Thy faith - ful mer - cies crown.
Let us all in Thee in - her - it, Let us find the prom - ised rest;
Sud - den - ly re - turn, and nev - er, Nev - er - more Thy tem - ples leave.
Let us see Thy great sal - va - tion Per - fect - ly re - stored in Thee:
Je - sus, Thou art all com - pas - sion, Pure, un - bound - ed love Thou art;
Take a - way our bent to sin - ning; Al - pha and O - me - ga be;
Thee we would be al - ways bless - ing, Serve Thee as Thy hosts a - bove,
Chang'd from glo - ry in - to glo - ry, Till in heav'n we take our place,
Vis - it us with Thy sal - va - tion; En - ter ev - 'ry trem - bling heart.
End of faith, as its be - gin - ning, Set our hearts at lib - er - ty.
Pray, and praise Thee with - out ceas - ing, Glo - ry in Thy per - fect love.
Till we cast our crowns be - fore Thee, Lost in won - der, love, and praise.

The 1879 Geo. Jardine & Son organ in Saint Patrick's Cathedral, New York

BIOGRAPHIES

BIOGRAPHIES

The **AEOLIAN EMPLOYEES' ASSOCIATION**, made up of Aeolianites in all departments of the company, was organized on February 15, 1916, and monthly meetings were held. At the meeting on April 10, 1916, attended by 500 employees, a musical program was presented that concluded with the new official song, *Our Company*, the singing of which "furnished a fair indication of the spirit of loyalty and sentiment which promoted the formation of the association." The anonymous text was set to the melody of the 16th-century Silesian folk song, "O Tannenbaum," familiar to the many German employees.

MARK ANDREWS, FAGO (1875–1939) immigrated to the United States from England in 1902 to become organist of St. Luke's Episcopal Church in Montclair, N.J. In 1912, he went to the First Baptist Church, and in 1917, the First Congregational Church where he remained for the rest of his life. A noted player, Andrews dedicated the Hope-Jones organ at Ocean Grove Auditorium in July 1908 and, between 1925 and 1928, he recorded 14 discs of hymns for Victor — sometimes with four hymns per disc. He composed more than three hundred organ works, songs, anthems, and secular choruses.

Born in Oxford, **FREDERIC ARCHER** (1838–1901) studied in Leipzig, and in 1873, was appointed organist of London's Alexandra Palace where he played more than two thousand recitals. He immigrated to New York in 1881 and played in churches there, Boston, and Chicago, before going to Pittsburgh as organist of the Carnegie Library and Music Hall and Church of the Ascension. In 1896, he organized the Pittsburgh Symphony.

AGNES ARMSTRONG, noted musicologist and acknowledged authority on the life and work Alexandre Guilmant, composed the winning hymn in a contest sponsored by the Council of Churches and the City of Albany for the official hymn of the Albany City Tercentennial in 1986. Texts proposed were three psalms chosen by the committee and Armstrong paraphrased Psalm 148.

A native of Brooklyn and a graduate of Fordham University, **ANTHONY BAGLIVI** (b. 1944) was for 29 years editor and advertising manager of *The American Organist*, the journal of the American Guild of Organists. In 2002, he received the AGO President's Award.

A graduate of Yale University, **EDWARD SHIPPEN BARNES** (1887–1958) was organist at the Church of the Incarnation, New York (1911–1912), Rutgers Presbyterian Church (1913–1924), St. Stephen's Episcopal Church, Philadelphia (1924–1938), and the First Presbyterian Church, Santa Monica, Calif. (1938–1958). He composed two organ symphonies and many miscellaneous organ works. In 1928, he set the present text from *The Everlasting Mercy* by England's Poet Laureate John Masefield.

HOMER NEWTON BARTLETT (1845–1920), was a noted song composer, though his opus list exceeds 270 numbers in most genres. A Founder of the American Guild of Organists, he was organist of Marble Collegiate Church (1866–1878) and then Madison Avenue Baptist Church (1878–1909).

AMY (Mrs. H.H.A.) BEACH (1864–1944) was a distinguished pianist and America's first successful female composer. Her 1892 *Gaelic Symphony* was the first symphony composed and published by an American woman. Although her principal residence was in Hillsborough, N.H., from 1916, she maintained an apartment in New York from the fall of 1930, chiefly to be near her close friend David McK. Williams, organist of St. Bartholomew's Church.

Born in Brooklyn, MATTHEW M. BELLOCCHIO (b. 1950) earned a degree in architecture from the Pratt Institute and a bachelor of arts in psychology from St Francis College. For 28 years, he was project manager with the Roche Organ Company in Taunton, Mass. Since 2003, he has been project manager and designer with the Andover Organ Company. A fellow of the American Institute of Organbuilders, Bellocchio has chaired the AIO Education Committee and served twice on its board of directors, most recently as president.

Having earned BA and MA degrees from Syracuse University, STEPHEN BEST (b.1946) has been Lecturer in Organ and Keyboard at Hamilton College since 1970. He is minister of music at First Presbyterian Church, Utica, New York, and a composer of both organ and choral music.

IN 1866, EDWARD MORRIS BOWMAN (1848–1913) went to New York City to study with William Mason (piano), and John Paul Morgan (organ and theory). For one year, he was organist of Trinity Church, Wall Street (1866–67). Organist for a time in Saint Louis, he studied in Germany, Paris, and London, and was the first American to earn the Associate diploma from the Royal College of Organists. He was organist of Peddie Memorial Baptist Church in Newark, N.J. (1887–95), chair of the music department of Vassar College (1891–1895), organist of the new Baptist Temple in Brooklyn (1895–1906), and organist of Calvary Baptist Church in New York City from 1906. In addition, Bowman was president of the Virgil Practice Clavier Mfg. Co. The author of the text, Sarah Josepha Hale, also wrote "Mary Had a Little Lamb," persuaded Abraham Lincoln to make Thanksgiving a national holiday, and edited 19th-century women's magazines, including *Godey's Lady's Book.*

Few hymn composers have the record of success of WILLIAM BATCHELDER BRADBURY (1816–1868). Immortalized by "Jesus loves me, this I know," many hymnals today still contain "He leadeth me," "Just as I am," "Sweet hour of prayer," "Savior, like a shepherd lead us," and "My hope is built on nothing less." While organist of Brooklyn's First Baptist Church, he began compiling the first of his 59 song books. He established the Bradbury Piano Company with his brother, and organized Juvenile Musical Festivals in which thousands of children participated.

Brooklyn-born **GEORGE F. BRISTOW** (1825–1898) studied with his father and was, for 36 years a violinist in the New York Philharmonic Society orchestra. He conducted two orchestras and was a great champion of American music. He was organist of several churches, including Church of the Divine Paternity in 1896. He composed three symphonies, an opera, an oratorio, cantatas, and in 1888, a *New and Improved Method for Reed or Cabinet Organ.*

Born in Hartford, Conn., **DUDLEY BUCK** (1839–1909) was one of the first American composers to achieve widespread recognition. After study in Germany and Paris, he returned to Hartford and published his *Motette Collection* (1864), and the first organ sonata by an American (1865). From 1869 to 1871 he was in Chicago and, after the Great Fire, moved to Boston where he was organist of St. Paul's Church and was on the faculty of the New England Conservatory. His last move was to Brooklyn where he was organist of St. Ann's Church (1875–77) and organist and choirmaster of Holy Trinity Church (1877–1902).

HARRY T. BURLEIGH (1866–1949) attended New York's National Conservatory of Music, where he developed a friendship with Antonin Dvořák, the school's director. In 1894, he became baritone soloist at St. George's Church, Stuyvesant Square, and in 1900 soloist at Temple Emanu-El. An accomplished composer, he had a contract with Ricordi in 1911 and was one of the company's editors for many years. Burleigh was the first to arrange spirituals as art songs, making them accessible to concert artists. His artistic arrangements are still frequently performed, notably his setting of "In Christ there is no East or West" that today appears in more than 70 hymnals.

U.C. BURNAP (1834–1900) was a prolific composer of hymn tunes and editor of three hymnals, including the 1869 *Hymns of the Church* for the Reformed Dutch Church, and, with John Knowles Paine, *Hymns and Songs of Praise* (1874). He combined the career of successful organist at Brooklyn's Church on the Heights for 37 years with that of a dry-goods merchant. In 1872, the University of the City of New York conferred on him the Doctor of Music degree. It was only after his suicide on December 8, 1900, when his burial certificate was filed, that his full name was known: Uzziah Cicero.

Born in Englewood, N.J., **WILLIAM SIDELL CHESTER** (1865–1900) graduated from the Stevens Institute of Technology in 1886, joined the C. & C. Electric Motor Company, and within a year had devised a way to apply electric motors to the pumping of organ bellows. Chester was appointed organist and choirmaster of St. George's Church, Stuyvesant Square, in 1888, where he directed the largest vested choir in the city, "a male choir of 55 voices [25 boys, 30 men] and an auxiliary choir of 20 female voices." Chester was a victim of typhoid fever and a volume of his *Hymn Tunes and Benedicite* was published by G. Schirmer as a memorial.

KATE SARA CHITTENDEN (1856–1949) studied at Hellmuth College in London, Ontario. She taught at Vassar College for 31 years (1890–ca. 1920) and was organist at Calvary Baptist in New York from 1879 until 1906. Chittenden originated the synthetic piano method, was one of the founders of the Metropolitan College of Music in New York, a Founder of the American Guild of Organists, and its librarian from 1899 to 1900. She was the first woman lecturer employed by the New York City board of education and served from 1892 to 1919. Her hymns were published by Silver, Burdett & Co. in 1894 in *The Calvary Hymnal.*

CARSON COOMAN (b. 1982) is a graduate of Harvard and Carnegie Mellon universities and is composer-in-residence of the Memorial Church at Harvard. A noted composer, he has written hundreds of works, from instrumental and orchestral pieces to operas.

While studying in England, **HENRY STEPHEN CUTLER** (1825–1902) fell under the influence of the Oxford Movement. After his return to Boston in 1846, he became organist of the Church of the Advent where he formed a vested choir of men and boys. When he was appointed organist of Trinity Church, New York, in 1858, he removed women from the choir and at the time of a visit by the Prince of Wales, introduced a vested men's choir in the chancel. His tune ALL SAINTS NEW was composed in 1872 for Reginald Heber's text, "The Son of God goes forth to war" and was published in the 1872 Episcopal hymnal.

LEOPOLD DAMROSCH (1832–1885) was a German violinist and conductor and an intimate of Liszt and Wagner. He who came to New York in 1871, founded the Oratorio Society in 1873, and four years later the Symphony Society. In September 1884, he was appointed general manager and chief conductor of the Metropolitan Opera, where he conducted the first American performances of many of Wagner's operas, including *Der Ring des Nibelungen.*

WALTER DAMROSCH (1862–1950) was the second son of Leopold Damrosch and one of America's most prodigious musicians who was recognized by millions when, as music director of the National Broadcasting Company, he hosted the *Music Appreciation Hour,* a popular series of radio lectures on classical music. He was his father's assistant as conductor of the Oratorio and Symphony societies, and the Metropolitan Opera. He was also organist for the Oratorio Society and, for one year, organist of Henry Ward Beecher's Plymouth Church. It was Damrosch who convinced Andrew Carnegie to build his New York Music Hall and who, having conducted the American premiere of Tchaikovsky's Fourth Symphony, invited the Russian composer to New York for the opening of Carnegie Hall in May 1891. He commissioned George Gershwin's Piano Concerto in F, conducted the premiere of *An American in Paris* and the premiere of Aaron Copeland's First Symphony, with Nadia Boulanger as organ soloist. The *Peace Hymn of the Republic,* set to a text by Henry Van Dyke (1852–1933), was published in 1919. It was sung by the audience at the dedication of the Kilgen organ in Carnegie Hall on November 4, 1929.

Though born in Middletown, Conn., **REGINALD DE KOVEN** (1859–1920) was graduated from Oxford at the age of 20 and then studied successively in Stuttgart, Frankfurt, Florence, Vienna, and Paris (with Léo Delibes). In addition to composing 20 operettas and more than 400 songs ("O Promise Me" is the most famous), he was a noted music critic for the *Chicago Evening Post, Harper's Weekly*, the *New York World*, and the *New York Herald*. Rudyard Kipling's poem, "Recessional" was written for Queen Victoria's Diamond Jubilee in 1897, celebrating the 60th anniversary of her reign.

VERNON DE TAR (1905–1999) was born in Detroit and studied piano and organ at Syracuse University, graduating in 1927. He was organist and choirmaster of New York's Calvary Church (1932–39) and Church of the Ascension (1939–81), and taught at Union Theological Seminary's School of Sacred Music (1945–72), and the Juilliard School (1947–82). Walt Whitman's *Leaves of Grass* was published in 1855 and, until his death, Whitman rewrote and added to it. "Pioneers, O Pioneers" was written in 1865 and first appeared in the 1867 fourth edition.

CLARENCE DICKINSON (1873–1969) was probably the most influential force in American church music for almost three generations, and there was hardly a Protestant church whose service was not influenced by his organ and choral editions. He served on the editorial boards of several denominations for hymnals, edited and arranged more than 100 sacred choruses, anthems, and carols, and transcribed some 50 works for organ. For 50 years Dickinson was organist of the Brick Church and organist, and music director at Union Theological Seminary, where, in 1928, founded the School of Sacred Music.

Composer of the popular seventh *Humoresque*, "Songs by mother taught me," the *Slavonic Dances, Stabat Mater*, nine symphonies, and nine operas, **ANTONIN DVOŘÁK** (1841–1904) moved to New York in 1892 to become director of the National Conservatory of Music, where he remained until 1895. In 1922, the song "Goin' Home" was adapted from the English horn solo of the Largo of "New World Symphony." The arranger, William Arms Fisher, one of Dvořák's pupils at the National Conservatory, described the melody as "a moving expression of that nostalgia of the soul all human beings feel. That the lyric opening theme of the Largo should spontaneously suggest the words 'Goin' home, goin' home' is natural enough, and that the lines that follow the melody should take the form of a spiritual accords with the genesis of the symphony."

A graduate of Hope College and Montclair State University, **ALFRED V. FEDAK,** FAGO (b. 1953) is a noted composer of church music with four anthologies of hymn tunes issued by Selah Publishing Co. Since 1990, he has been minister of music and arts at Westminster Presbyterian Church in Albany. He is also organist and choir director of Congregation Beth Emeth in Albany.

CARYL FLORIO (1843–1920) was born William James Robjohn in Tavistock, England. His father William Robjohn immigrated to America with his family in 1858, and joined his brother Thomas in an organbuilding business. The son sang in the choir of Trinity Church (1859–60) and was its first solo boy soprano when Stephen Cutler dismissed the women singers. Robjohn followed the career of a professional musician: teacher, organist, choral and opera conductor, translator, accompanist, pianist, music critic, editor, and composer. A career all the more amazing considering that, except for a few early music lessons, he was entirely self-taught. Ostensibly, Robjohn's family objected to his choice of a musical career, and in 1870, he adopted the pseudonym Caryl Florio. He was organist of several New York churches, including the Brick Church. Florio settled in North Carolina, where, from 1896 until 1901, he was in charge of the music at George W. Vanderbilt's estate, BILTMORE, near Asheville, and organist and choirmaster of All Souls' Church on the estate. He composed many hymns, the excellence of which made the decision of including just one, difficult.

STEPHEN COLLINS FOSTER (1826–1864), "The Father of American Music," wrote, within his short life, some of the most memorable songs in American history, including "Jeanie with the light brown hair," "Beautiful dreamer," "My old Kentucky home," and "Old folks at home," to mention but four. Though well educated, Foster taught himself to play several instruments and had no formal instruction in composition. He lived most of his life in Pittsburgh, where he was born, but spent the last four years of his life in New York City in obscurity, and after a fall in a Bowery hotel, died in Bellevue Hospital at the age of 37. Thomas M. Walker, in his 1909 *The Melodies of Stephen C. Foster* (which contains 15 hymns), wrote that Foster was a member of the Episcopal Church and was deeply religious.

GIDEON FROELICH was born between 1845 and 1847 in Hungary or Germany. He was organist of Fifth Avenue Baptist Church in New York City in 1886 and later of Brooklyn's Hanson Place Baptist Church. For many years, he was organist of Ahawath Chesed Synagogue. The rabbi, Isaac S. Moses, edited *The Sabbath-School Hymnal*, the seventh edition of which was published in 1906. He was also rabbi of Central Synagogue for 17 years and author of the prayer book used in most reformed synagogues in America.

CLEMENT ROWLAND GALE (1862–1934) was born in Kew, England, and graduated from Exeter College, Oxford in arts (1884) and music (1889). He was music-master at the Reading School (1884–85) and sub-organist of St. Mary's Cathedral, Edinburgh (1885–89). Gale immigrated to New York in 1890 and was organist of Calvary Church (1890–1900), All Angels' (1900–10), and Christ Church. He was organist and instructor at General Theological Seminary from 1901, and an instructor in harmony, counterpoint, and composition at the Guilmant Organ School from 1902.

AUGUSTA BROWNE GARRETT (1820–1882) was born in Dublin, Ireland, and her family immigrated to the United States by the time she was ten years old. She was organist of the First Presbyterian Church in Brooklyn during the 1840s and '50s. At the time of her death she was one of the more prolific women composers in the country, having written more than 200 salon piano pieces and drawing-room songs — all the while resisting the vernacular American styles that she described as "taste-corrupting." By the late 1840s, Garrett had become a prominent author, writing two books and contributing musical articles to popular magazines. "I have a glorious hope!" appeared in the March 1880 issue of *Frank Leslie's Sunday Magazine,* the title being "the expression of a dying Christian, eighty-two years of age."

A graduate and faculty member of Baltimore's Peabody Conservatory, **ARCHER GIBSON** (1875–1952) was brought to New York in 1901 by Maltie Babcock when he was called as pastor to New York's Brick Church. Gibson was held in esteem by the musicians of New York (he also passed the first Fellowship examination given by the American Guild of Organists in 1902), and within three years had embarked on a career as a residence organist, playing the new Aeolian organs in the palatial homes of the wealthy. Gibson recorded 72 Duo-Art organ rolls for the Aeolian Company, and 18 sides of RCA Victor phonograph discs. The words of "This happy Christmas morning" were written by Ida Scott Taylor (not to be confused with the pseudonym of Fanny Crosby) who married William E. McKinney (1852–1936), a brick and tile manufacturer in De Witt, Iowa.

Architect, preservationist, and organist, **SEBASTIAN M. GLÜCK** (b. 1960) is also a New York organbuilder — president and tonal director of Glück Pipe Organs, established in 1985. He was on the OHS Publications Governing Board as well as the committee on Guidelines for Restoration and Conservation. Glück has been a member of the Executive Board of the New York City Chapter of the American Guild of Organists and in 2007, chaired the Region II AGO Convention.

Born in New Orleans, **LOUIS MOREAU GOTTSCHALK** (1829–1869) was a child prodigy who entered the Paris Conservatory at the age of 13. After a concert at Salle Pleyel, Chopin predicted that Gottschalk would "become the king of pianists." Upon his return to the United States in 1853, Gottschalk toured constantly and became America's most famous composer and pianist. During a concert in Rio de Janeiro, he collapsed, having contracted yellow fever, and died three weeks later on December 18, 1869, in a hotel, probably from an overdose of quinine. His funeral was held on October 3, 1870 at St. Stephen's Church with George Washbourn Morgan attending, George William Warren as a pall bearer, and William Berge as the organist. His popular piano caprice, *The Last Hope,* became so popular that by 1862 it had sold more than 35,000 copies and Gottschalk was obliged to repeat it at every concert. Two years before his death, it had been arranged as a hymn, GOTTSCHALK, and appeared in a Methodist hymnal. In 1878, a third version, MERCY, was published, which is the one sung today.

The brilliant Australian pianist **PERCY ALDRIDGE GRANGER** (1882–1961) began his first American tour on February 11, 1915, with a recital at New York's Aeolian Hall (he later recorded 48 Duo-Art piano rolls for the Aeolian Company). A naturalized citizen in 1918, he maintained a residence in White Plains, and from 1932 to 1933, was head of the music department of New York University.

Born at Burton-on-Trent, England, **HENRY W. GREATOREX** (1811–1858) immigrated to Hartford, Conn., in 1839 and was organist of Center Church (First Congregational) and St. John's Episcopal Church, West Hartford. By 1846, he was organist of St. Paul's in New York, when, with several other organists, he exhibited the new Erben organ at Trinity Church on October 7 and 8. In 1850, Greatorex went to Calvary Church, New York, as organist and choirmaster. The next year he published *A Collection of Psalm and Hymn Tunes, Chants, Anthems, and Sentences,* the aim of which being "to furnish good music, rather than light, frivolous melody . . . [and] to avoid vulgarity, or straining after effect." His hymns are among the finest examples of the genre, and that included here is distinguished in the third phrase by a descending scale of two and one-half octaves passed among the lower voices. After three years, Greatorex left Calvary Church and, in 1853, moved to Charleston, S.C., where he was organist of the new Catholic Cathedral of St. John and St. Finbar, Kahal Kadosh Beth Elohim Synagogue, and later of St. Philip's Church. He died of yellow fever, September 10, 1858.

A student of Michael Schneider on a Fulbright grant, **FREDERICK GRIMES** (b. 1941) was organist and director of music at Holy Trinity Lutheran Church in New York from 1970 to 1992 where he led one of the country's unique music programs, presenting a Bach cantata every Sunday afternoon. For 25 years, he has been organist and choirmaster of All Saints' Church, Fort Worth.

HENRY K. HADLEY (1971–1937) studied in Vienna, and upon returning to the United States taught music at St. Paul's School for Boys in Garden City, N.Y., from 1896 until 1902. He was organist of All Souls' Unitarian Church and in 1900 made his conducting debut at the Waldorf-Astoria hotel in a program of his own works. He was conductor of the Seattle Symphony (1909–11) and the first conductor of the San Francisco Symphony (1911–15). In 1921, he became associate conductor of the New York Philharmonic. Hadley was one of the most performed American composers of his day, his opera *Cleopatra's Night* being premiered at the Metropolitan Opera on January 31, 1920.

FRANK SEYMOUR HASTINGS (1853–1924) was the grandson of Thomas Hastings, composer of "Rock of Ages," son of Thomas Samuel (graduate, professor of sacred rhetoric and pastoral theology, and president of Union Theological Seminary — for whom Hastings Hall is named), and brother of architect Thomas Hastings of Carrière and Hastings. Throughout his career, Frank Hastings was associated with oil refining companies and banks, a confidential adviser to J.P. Morgan, and executor of Grover Cleveland's estate. He was a devoted music patron who endowed the MacDowell Memorial Association, was a director of the Oratorio Society, and president of the Russian Symphony Society. His song, "A Red, Red Rose" was popular at one time and on April 19, 1905, his cantata *The Temptation,* was given privately at Aeolian Hall, sung by soloists and members of the Brooklyn Amateur Musical Club.

THOMAS HASTINGS (1784–1872) was a self-taught musician who began his career as a singing teacher in Clinton, New York. In 1831, he published a hymnbook compiled with Lowell Mason that included his most famous hymn, "Rock of Ages." Hastings worked in New York City churches from 1832 until his death. In 1822, he published the first musical treatise by an American author, *Dissertation on Musical Taste,* which was influential in shifting American music from British to German models.

EDWARD HODGES (1796–1867) earned the Doctor of Music degree from Cambridge University and immigrated to Canada in 1838 where he was appointed organist of Toronto Cathedral. He soon moved to New York where he became organist of St. John's Chapel and, in 1846, of Trinity Church, which opened its third building on May 21.

Born in Bristol, **JOHN SEBASTIAN BACH HODGES** (1830–1915) was the son of Edward Hodges. In 1845, he immigrated to New York, attended Columbia University and General Theological Seminary, and was ordained an Episcopal minister in 1854. He was a curate at Grace Church, Newark (1860–1870), and then rector of St. Paul's Church, Baltimore, for 35 years. His 1868 *Book of Common Praise* was a companion to the *Book of Common Prayer.* Always associated with the text, "Bread of the world, in mercy broken," Hodges's most popular hymn tune was alternately known as PANIS VITAE.

Professor of sacred music and director of chapel music at New York's General Theological Seminary for 28 years, **DAVID HURD** (b. 1950) is now director of music at the Church of Saint Mary the Virgin. In 1977, he received first prizes in both organ performance and improvisation from the International Congress of Organists, the only person to ever win both prizes in the same year. He has more than 100 choral and organ works in print, many contributions to the *Hymnal 1982,* and his *Intercession Mass* is sung in hundreds of churches throughout America.

A noted pianist and composer, **HENRY HOLDEN HUSS** (1862–1953) was born in Newark, N.J. He studied first with his father, and later, organ and composition with Josef Rheinberger at the Munich Conservatory (1882–85). He was organist of various churches in New York City and taught at the Masters School (1897–1932) and Hunter College from 1931.

JOHN ALBERT JEFFERY (1855–1929) immigrated to America in 1876 and settled in Albany, N.Y., where he was organist of the Cathedral of All Saints. ANCIENT OF DAYS was written for the Bicentenary of the City of Albany in 1886. The words are by William Doane, then Bishop of Albany. In 1893, Jeffery was organist of the First Presbyterian Church, Yonkers, N.Y., and later taught music at the New England Conservatory.

DION W. KENNEDY (1882–1946) was Archer Gibson's assistant at the Brick Church and then organist of Brooklyn's Church of the Pilgrims (1909–1911) and the Church of the New Jerusalem, Swedenborgian, in Manhattan. He was one of the Aeolian Company's valued organ salesmen. Kennedy later moved to Montecito, California, where, for seven years before his death he was organist and choirmaster of All Saints-by-the-Sea Episcopal Church.

In 1834, **WILLIAM A. KING** (1817–1867) emigrated from England at the age of 17 and amazed New York audiences with his virtuosic concert paraphrases on American patriotic songs. His *Brilliant Fantasia on "Hail Columbia"* and *Grand National Fantasy on "The Star Spangled Banner"* brought him fame as the foremost pianist in America. He was organist of Grace Church (1839–1855), Calvary (1857/58–1860), St. George's, and other New York churches, and, with George Washbourn Morgan, was considered the foremost organist in the United States. He was found by a policeman lying dead on the sidewalk near the corner of Fourth Avenue and 31st Street, Saturday morning, May 11, 1867, "the result of excessive intemperance." His *Grace Church Collection* and *King's New Collection* were "highly esteemed by eminent quartet choirs."

BRUNO OSCAR KLEIN (1858–1911) came TO America in 1878, toured as a concert pianist, and was, for a time, organist of St. John's Cathedral in Quincy, Illinois. Moving to New York City, he was organist of the Church of St. Francis Xavier (1884–94) and of St. Ignatius Loyola (1904–11). Klein was head of the piano department at the Convent of the Sacred Heart (1884–1911) and taught counterpoint and composition at the National Conservatory (1887–92). "By Thy thirst at Jacob's well," a fine example of a Roman Catholic temperance hymn, was composed for the 1896 *League Hymnal: A Collection of Sacred Heart Hymns.*

Born in New York City, **PHOEBE PALMER** (1839–1908) married Joseph Knapp, one of the founders and second president of the Metropolitan Life Insurance Company. They were members of the John Street Methodist Episcopal Church and, coincidentally, so was their friend, hymn writer Fanny Crosby. Phoebe Knapp's most familiar hymn is "Blessed Assurance," set to lyrics by Fannie Crosby and her Palm Sunday sacred song "Open the Gates of the Temple" (also with words by Fannie Crosby), was once almost as popular as Faure's "The Palms."

LAAST UNS ERFREUEN is a 1623 German hymn tune, harmonized by Ralph Vaughan Williams, and first published in the 1906 *English Hymnal.* The text is by Cyril Argentine Alington (1872–1955), a prolific British author and educator who was chaplain to King George V (1921–33) and dean of Durham Cathedral (1933–51). New York's Trinity Church, Wall Street, was dedicated on Ascension Day, May 21, 1846, and, since the two events coincided, the Feast of the Ascension has always been a brilliant liturgical celebration augmented with orchestra. The procession was the March of the Templars, "O Zion! Blest City," from Henry Hiles's *The Crusaders,* and until 1966, the Gradual Hymn was "Praise Him, ye architects who planned," sung to the same tune as "Ye watchers and ye holy ones." It is not known if the text were written specifically for Trinity Church.

Philadelphia-born **ROBERT LOWRY** (1826–1899) was a Baptist minister who was pastor of Bloomingdale Baptist Church, New York (1858–61), Brooklyn's Hanson

Place Baptist Church (1861–69), and later of what became known as Park Avenue Baptist Church. He edited some 18 gospel song books, his second, *Bright Jewels,* sold half a million copies in four years from its publication in 1869, and the third, *Pure Gold,* sold more than a million by 1888. "Shall we gather at the river" was written in Brooklyn in July 1864 and is based on Revelations 22:1, "And he shewed me a pure river of water of life, clear as crystal, proceeding out of the throne of God and of the Lamb."

WILLIAM CHARLES MACFARLANE (1870–1945) was organist in New York at All Souls' Church (1889–1900), Temple Emanu-El (1898–1912), and St. Thomas Church (1900–12). He went to Portland, Maine, as municipal organist in 1912, remaining until 1919. Macfarlane was a well-known choral composer, his most famous anthem being "Open Our Eyes."

J. CHRISTOPHER MARKS (1863–1946) was born in Cork, Ireland, and studied with his father, for 43 years organist of Cork Cathedral. After 21 years as organist of St. Luke's Episcopal Church in Cork (1881–1902), Marks immigrated to Pittsburgh in 1902 and became organist of St. Andrew's Church. Two years later he moved to New York to become organist of Church of the Heavenly Rest, where he remained until 1929.

EDUARDO MARZO (1852–1929) was born in Naples, came to America at the age of 15, and toured as accompanist for prominent singers and the great violinist Pablo Sarasate. He held several church positions in New York City: St. Agnes R.C. (1887), St. Ann's R.C. (1890–93), All Saints' R.C. (1894), Church of the Ascension, Episcopal (1896), Church of the Holy Name R.C. (1918–), and Holy Spirit R.C. (1929). An editor for G. Schirmer for many years, Marzo was also a prolific composer of music for both Roman Catholic and Protestant services as well as secular songs and operettas.

LOWELL MASON (1792–1872) is regarded as the "Father of American Church Music." At the age of 20, as a clerk in a Savannah, Ga., bank, he studied composition with Frederick L. Abel and compiled his first collection of church music, which contained many of his own compositions. It was finally published in Boston in 1822 as *The Handel and Haydn Society Collection of Church Music.* Among his more popular hymns were "Joy to the World," "Nearer my God to Thee", "When I survey the wondrous cross", and "My faith looks up to Thee." In 1855, Mason was awarded an honorary doctorate in music from Yale University, to which school he later gave his vast collection of books and music.

ARTHUR HENRY MESSITER (1834–1916) was educated by private tutors in England. He immigrated to the United States in 1863, was organist of St. James the Less in Philadelphia, and in 1866, succeeded Henry Cutler as organist and choirmaster of Trinity Church, New York. He was an editor of the *Episcopal Hymnal* (1893), compiled the *Psalter* (1889) and *Choir Office Book* (1891), and wrote *A History of the Choir and Music if Trinity Church, New York* (1906). MARION, composed in 1884 and named for his wife, was published in Messiter's 1893 *Hymnal with Music as Used in Trinity Church.*

HARRISON MILLARD (1830–1895) was a famous songwriter, voice teacher, and nationally known concert singer. At the age of 15, he sang alto in Boston's Handel and Haydn Society. His song "Viva L'America," written in 1861, was his greatest success and was played for Lincoln at the Washington Naval Yard that year. Millard was a First Lieutenant in the U.S. infantry during the Civil War, saw four years of combat, and was severely wounded at Chickamauga in 1863. He returned to New York and worked for 21 years as a U.S. Customs clerk, during which time he was tenor soloist at St. Stephen's R.C. Church. He wrote about 350 songs, in addition to anthems, four Episcopal services, four Te Deum settings, a Grand Mass in G, and an opera to an Italian libretto, *Deborah.*

Born in Gloucester, England, **GEORGE WASHBOURN MORGAN** (1823–1892), was a prominent organist by the age of 20 and, after positions in Cheltenham and London, immigrated to New York in December 1853. He was organist of St. Thomas Church (1854), Grace Church (1855–68), St. Ann's R.C. Church (1868–69), St. Stephen's R.C. Church (1869–70), the Brooklyn Tabernacle (1870–82), and other churches in Manhattan and New Jersey. In 1880, Morgan, joined by his 20-year-old daughter, instituted a series of five Lenten organ and harp matinées at Chickering Hall that continued for twelve years. It was as America's first traveling organ virtuoso that Morgan became famous. It was said that having an organ inauguration without Morgan was like a performance of Shakespeare's *Hamlet* with Hamlet left out. Though he was the first to play Bach fugues and the organ works of Mendelssohn in America, it was his performance of the *William Tell Overture* that earned him a phenomenal reputation and was always requested.

JOHN PAUL MORGAN (1841–1879) was the son of John Morgan, DD, one of the professors of Cincinnati's Lane Seminary who left in 1834 because anti-slavery discussion was prohibited, and founded the Oberlin Theological Seminary. His son was graduated from Oberlin College and studied at the Leipzig Conservatory and with August Gottfried Ritter. He returned to Oberlin in August 1865, founded the Conservatory of Music and directed it through the first year. In 1866, he moved to New York and, after a year as organist of Brooklyn's Church of the Messiah, was appointed assistant organist of Trinity Church at Easter 1867. With Arthur Messiter, he induced the vestry to establish the orchestral service at Trinity and orchestrated many English anthems. In 1873, a throat infection caused him to resign from Trinity and move to Santa Barbara, Calif. He was conductor there of the Handel and Haydn Society of San Francisco and the Oakland Harmonic Society and organist of the First Presbyterian Church in Oakland. In September 1877, he founded the Morgan Conservatory of Music.

JOSEPH MOSENTHAL (1834–1896) was born in Kassel, Germany, studied with Ludwig Spohr and, for four years, played second violin in the Kassel court orchestra under Spohr. In 1853, he immigrated to New York where he was a member of the

Mason-Thomas Quintet (1855–68), and a violinist in the New York Philharmonic Orchestra for 40 years. He was organist of St. John's Church (185?–1859), and Calvary Church (1860–87). He was a strong proponent of the mixed-voiced choir and solo quartet, and was forced out of both posts when boy choirs were instituted. At the time of his death, he was organist of All Souls' Unitarian Church. Mosenthal conducted the Mendelssohn Glee Club from 1867 and members thought so much of him that in 1893 they paid $1,000 to have his portrait painted by John White Alexander.

> On a blustering night in January 1896, Joseph Mosenthal fought against the elements in his effort to reach the rehearsal in Mendelssohn Hall and stumbling into the room, exhausted and overcome by his exertion, he was gently laid on a sofa directly under his own portrait and there, half an hour later, he died surrounded by the members.

"Still thy sorrow, Magdalena!" is an ancient Latin hymn, "Pone luctum, Magdalena!" translated by E.A. Washburn in June 1868. It was included in Mosenthal's *Christmas and Easter Carols Prepared for the Sunday Schools of Calvary Church and Chapel* (1878) and later appeared as the tune ROSSTHWAITE in *The Church Hymnary* in 1908.

WILLIAM HAROLD NEIDLINGER (1863–1924) was born in Brooklyn, where he studied with Dudley Buck, and later taught in the music department of the Brooklyn Institute of Arts and Sciences. He was organist of St. Michael's Episcopal Church, Manhattan. He studied in London and Paris from 1896 until 1901 and, on his return to the United States, settled in Chicago where he was a successful singing teacher. After the success of his *Small Songs for Small Singers,* intended for children in kindergarten, he became interested in child psychology, and eventually opened a school for children with special needs in East Orange, New Jersey. His fame rests on his 1890 Christmas song, "The Birthday of a King."

HORACE WADHAM NICHOLL (1848–1922) was born at Tipton, near Birmingham, England, and held positions at Dudley and at Stoke-on-Trent from 1867 to 1871, when he was induced by an American gentleman to accompany him to Pittsburgh, where became organist of St. Paul's Cathedral, and later at the Third Presbyterian Church. In 1878, he went to New York, where he became organist of St. Mark's Church. Nicholl was an active writer on music as well as a composer, and his articles and letters frequently appeared in the *Musical Courier,* the *American Musician,* and the *Art Journal;* he also was an editor at Schuberth and at Schirmer and wrote music textbooks. Nicholl wrote one of the first cello sonatas known to be composed in the United States. The text of PRINCETON is the twelfth stanza of *The Builders,* an Academic Ode by Henry Van Dyke, minister of New York's Brick Church. He recited it in Alexander Hall at the 150th anniversary of Princeton College, October 21, 1896. It appeared in several magazines and was subsequently published in *The Builders and Other Poems.*

After studying at the Royal College of Music, T. TERTIUS NOBLE (1867–1953) was first organist and choirmaster of Ely Cathedral (1892–98) and then of York Minster (1898–1913). After a recital tour of the United States he succeeded Will C. Macfarlane as organist of St. Thomas Church, New York, in 1913 and remained until 1943. Several of his anthems were popular for many years, including "Souls of the Righteous," "Fierce Was the Wild Billow," and "Go to Dark Gethsemane." A prolific hymn tune composer, seven of his melodies are included in the *Hymnal 1940*. His most popular tune is ORA LABORA.

HOMER NORRIS (1860–1920) was a graduate of the New England Conservatory and spent four years in Paris studying with Guilmant, Gigout, and Dubois. After positions in Maine and Boston, he was organist of St. George's from 1904 until he moved to California in 1913. J. Pierpont Morgan, senior warden of St. George's, built for Norris a $20,000 stone castle, "The Boulders," high on a crag of the Orange Mountains facing Greenwood Lake. Upon being struck by a taxicab in front of Carnegie Hall on June 20, 1920, Norris's right leg was broken above the knee. Blood poisoning subsequently set in, and he died in Roosevelt Hospital two months later.

One of the popular traditions in New York on Palm Sunday in the early 20th century was attending St. George's Church, Stuyvesant Square, to hear Harry T. Burleigh sing *The Palms* of Faure and Homer Norris's version of the hymn, "Ride on! Ride on in majesty," set to the King's Song, "Des Reinen Arm gieb Heldenkraft" (Give him who's pure heroic strength) from Act 1, Scene 3 of Richard Wagner's *Lohengrin.*

GEORGE EDGAR OLIVER (1856–1941) was a theater manager, drama critic, and director of music for the public school system of Albany, N.Y. He attended the Albany Classical Institute, and later the Albany Academy, from which he graduated in 1872. He attended Harvard, but because of poor eyesight, had to withdraw and he subsequently took up music. He was organist at All Saints Cathedral, Emanuel Baptist Church, Second Presbyterian Church, and St. Paul's Episcopal Church in Albany. He taught three generations of students, and it was said he never forgot the first names of his thousands of pupils.

Born in the Ukranian province of Poltava, LEO ORNSTEIN (1895–2002) was a musical child prodigy and by the age of eight was studying composition with Alexander Glazunov and piano with Anna Yesipova at the Moscow Conservatory. The family immigrated to the United States in 1906 and he made his debut as a pianist in 1911. He was at the forefront of the modern musical movement, a "futurist," and was the first composer to make extensive use of tone clusters. After a controversial career, he retired from public life in that late 1930s. In 1929, Ornstein's hymn, and the text by Frederick H. Martens (best known as the author of the words to Pietro Yon's *Gesù Bambino*), won the $3,000 first prize in Florence Brooks-Aten's competition for a new national anthem.

HORATIO WILLIAM PARKER (1863–1919) studied with George Chadwick in Boston and for three years, with Josef Rheinberger in Munich. He held Episcopal church positions at St. Luke's, Brooklyn (1885), St. Andrew's, Harlem (1887), Holy Trinity, Manhattan (1888), Trinity Church, Boston (1893–1901), and St. Nicholas, Manhattan (1901). In 1894, Parker was appointed the first chairman of the music department at Yale University, where his composition students included Charles Ives, Roger Sessions, Seth Bingham, and Quincy Porter. Horatio Parker was an internationally successful American composer at the turn of the 20th century. His oratorio, *Hora Novissima,* one of the most widely-sung choral works of the time, was performed at the Three Choirs Festival in England, and his opera *Mona* was produced at the Metropolitan Opera in 1912. He composed some 36 organ works, including a sonata and the first organ concerto by an American. He was a talented composer of hymn tunes, with nine in the 1894 and 1916 Episcopal hymnals, and five in the *Hymnal 1940.*

Born in London, **STEPHEN AUSTEN PEARCE** (1836–1900) earned a Mus.D. at Oxford University, immigrated to America in 1872, and succeeded his brother, James, as organist of St. Mark's Church, Philadelphia. He remained only one year and left to become organist of Christ Church, New York, later moving to St. George's Church, Stuyvesant Square. In January 1876, he was among the prominent organists who exhibited the new Roosevelt organ in Chickering Hall. Pearce later played at the Fifth Avenue Collegiate Dutch Church (1882), St. Stephen's R.C. (1893), Church of the Ascension, and First Presbyterian Church, Jersey City, where he died after the Sunday morning service, on April 9, 1900. He taught voice at Columbia College, lectured at other schools, and was music editor of the *New York Evening Post.*

Born in Yates, a town in northwest New York bordering Lake Ontario, **WILLIAM S. PITTS** (1830–1918) lived most of this life in Fredericksburg, Iowa. At the age of 35, he moved to Chicago to attend medical school and sold his song, "There's a church in the valley of the wildwood," to a publisher for $25 to pay the enrollment fee. He practiced medicine in Fredericksburg until 1906 when he moved to Brooklyn to be near his son.

BRONSON RAGAN (1915–1971) was a native of Rome, N.Y., and studied with David McK. Williams and Gaston Dethier at the Juilliard School of Music. He joined the Juilliard faculty in 1938 and also taught at the Guilmant Organ School and Union Theological Seminary's School of Sacred Music. We are grateful to Kevin Walters for providing a copy of Ragan's hymn tune.

MCNEIL ROBINSON (1943–2015) was a graduate of the Juilliard School and chair of the organ department at the Manhattan School of Music (1991–2015). He was organist of the Church of St. Mary the Virgin (1965–82), the Church of the Holy Family (United Nations), Park Avenue Christian Church to 2008, Park Avenue Synagogue (1965–2012), and Holy Trinity R.C. Church (2008–2014). Works were commissioned from him for three national AGO conventions: San Francisco (1984), Boston (1990), and New York City (1996). THURMAN was commissioned by the Irvington Presbyterian Church, Irvington-on-Hudson, N.Y., in celebration of the tenth anniversary of F. Anthony Thurman's music ministry, and was premiered on May 23, 2004.

After organ positions in Boston, **GEORGE F. ROOT** (1820–1895) helped to establish the New York Normal Musical Institute. There he met Fanny Crosby who wrote the words for more than 60 of his popular songs. Root was particularly successful composing Civil War songs, "Tramp! Tramp! Tramp!" being his most famous. The SHINNING SHORE was Henry Ward Beecher's favorite hymn and, "on occasions when he knew distinguished strangers to be in the congregation or had any minister from a distance with him in the pulpit, he was apt to allow the people to exhibit their vocal power by singing it." The first verse was by abolitionist David Nelson.

CHARLES BLACKMER RUTENBER (1849–1918) was born in Newburgh, N.Y. He appears to have come to New York City in the 1880s and was organist of St. Andrew's P.E. Church, Harlem in 1884. He was on the faculty of the Metropolitan Conservatory of Music when it was founded in 1886, and organist and choir director of the Collegiate Reformed Church of Harlem in 1889. Rutenber also conducted choral societies in Poughkeepsie and Newburgh. On May 1, 1902, he became organist of the Congregational Church in Poughkeepsie, but he left in the spring of 1904. In 1908, Rutenber published *Hymns of the Riven Rock,* intended to "cover the needs, both of evangelistic services, missionary meetings, and meetings for the promotion of deeper spiritual life."

SUMNER SALTER (1856–1944) graduated from Amherst College in 1877 and studied privately with Benjamin D. Allen and Eugene Thayer (organ), and John Knowles Paine (theory). He was organist successively of the First Unitarian Church, Lynn, and Eliot Congregational Church, Roxbury, Mass.; he was organist of Cleveland's Euclid Avenue Baptist Church, and taught at the Oberlin Conservatory (1879–81). Salter was organist of St. Paul's, Syracuse, N.Y. (1881–86), First Methodist, Atlanta, Ga. (1886–89), and from 1889 to 1900 in New York City at the First Presbyterian Church and at West End Avenue Collegiate Church. He was organist at Cornell University and teacher of voice at the Ithaca Conservatory (1900–2), organist of the Broadway Tabernacle, New York City (1902–5), and organist at Williams College from 1905.

Born in Utica, N.Y., CARL G. SCHMIDT (1868–1938) spent his musical career in Brooklyn, where he worked for the public school system for 26 years, eventually becoming chairman of the music department of Erasmus Hall High School. He was organist of New York Avenue Methodist Church, and later of Central Presbyterian Church. Schmidt was also director of sight-singing at the Brooklyn Institute of Arts and Sciences and president of the Brooklyn Oratorio Society. The text, "Quæ stella sole pulchrior," is a Vesper Hymn by Charles Coffin (1676–1749) published in the *Paris Breviary* (1736).

HARRY ROWE SHELLEY (1858–1947) was one of the more successful composers of church music at the turn of the 20th century, his most famous anthem, *Hark! Hark, My Soul,* had sold more than 31,000 copies by the time of his death. Shelley was Charles Ives's composition teacher, and the manuscript of Ives's *Variations on "America"* bears his corrections. Born in New Haven, by the age of 14, Shelley played the organ at Center Church on the Green and studied with Gustav Stoeckel, the Yale chapel organist. He entered Yale University but withdrew during his first year to study music full-time. He studied with Dudley Buck, Max Vogrich, and with

Antonin Dvořák at the National Conservatory of Music. Shelley was organist of Brooklyn's Church of the Pilgrims (1878–85, 1887–1896), Plymouth Church (1885–87), Fifth Avenue Baptist, Manhattan (1896–1914), and Clinton Avenue Congregational Church (1914–35).

WILLIAM FISK SHERWIN (1826–1888) was born, in Buckland, Mass., studied music with Lowell Mason and later became an instructor at the New England Conservatory. He was the first music director of the camp founded in 1874 for Sunday school teachers on the shores of Lake Chautauqua in western New York. The camp soon became the famous Chautauqua Institution and Sherwin remained with it for many years. He is known today for two hymn tunes written on texts by Mary Lathbury: "Break thou the bread of life" and "Day is dying in the west." Sherwin was also a musical editor for the Century Company and Biglow & Main, who published many of his songs.

HAMPSON A. SISLER, MD, FAGO (b. 1932) was born in Yonkers, N.Y. A child prodigy, he studied organ with David McK. Williams and Norman Coke-Jephcott, earned a licentiate from Trinity College, London, at the age of 16, and at 17 was the youngest person to earn the Fellowship certificate of the American Guild of Organists. In addition to being one of New York's most respected ophthalmologists, Sisler is a distinguished composer and has been organist and choirmaster at many prominent New York churches.

Born in Hagerstown, Md., **GERRIT SMITH** (1859–1912) is considered the Founder of the American Guild of Organists — it was he who suggested the name. He was organist of St. Paul's Cathedral, Buffalo, and St. Peter's Church, Albany, for a short time. In 1880, he went to Berlin to study with August Haupt and Eduard Rohde. From 1885 until he death, Smith was organist of South (Dutch Reformed) Church in New York City. He also taught theory at the Masters School in Brooklyn and was, for many years, music director at Union Theological Seminary. He composed anthems and songs, and left two collections of carols: *Ten Christmas Carols* and *Ten Easter Carols for Children.*

ROLLIN SMITH (b. 1942) is the OHS director of publications and editor of *The Tracker.* After his doctoral dissertation at the Juilliard School was published, he added writing about organ music to playing it, and his books on César Franck, Saint-Saëns, Vierne, and Stokowski have become the standard works on the subjects. In 2016, Smith was awarded the Nicholas Bessaraboff Prize by the American Musical Instrument Society for his *Pipe Organs of the Rich and Famous.* The second edition of his *The Aeolian Pipe Organ and Its Music* has just been published.

Born at Newburgh-on-Hudson, N.Y., **FANNY MORRIS SPENCER** (1867–193?) studied piano in New York City with Alexander Lambert, and organ and composition with Samuel P. Warren. She was organist of Pilgrim Congregational, Lexington Avenue Baptist, and Fourth Presbyterian churches, and on the faculty of Miss Spence's School for Girls in New York, Dr. Holbrook's Military School, and Miss Fuller's

School for Girls in Ossining. Spencer was considered one of the leading concert organists in the United States. a Founder of the American Guild of Organists, and gave two recitals in the Temple of Music at the 1901 Buffalo Pan-American Exposition. Her *Thirty-Two Hymns with Original Tunes* was published in 1893 by Novello, Ewer & Co.

MAX SPICKER (1858–1912) was born in Königsberg and studied at the Leipzig Conservatory with Carl Reinecke and Ernst Friedrich Richter. He immigrated to New York in 1882 and was an editor for G. Schirmer — his edition of Handel's *Messiah,* being ubiquitous in the United States. His two sacred solos, "Fear Not, Oh Israel" and "Why Are Thou Cast Down, My Soul?" were sung for many years in churches and synagogues. Choir director at Temple Emanu-El for many years, Spicker's funeral took place there on the morning of October 17, 1912.

LEOPOLD STOKOWSKI (1882–1977) was the icon of classical music for most of the 20th century. Born in London, he graduated from the Royal College of Music and earned the Fellowship diploma from the Royal College of Organists. He was brought to New York in 1905 by the rector of St. Bartholomew's Church to implement a vested choir of men and boys, but the plan was vetoed by the vestry, and the professional adult choir was retained. After three years as a successful church musician, Stokowski left to embark on a career as an orchestral conductor, first in Cincinnati (1909–12) and then in Philadelphia (1912–39). Subsequently he guest conducted most of the world's orchestras, appeared in four films, and enjoyed a 60-year recording career — the longest of any artist in history — making more recordings than any orchestral conductor. Stokovski's *Processional Hymn* (he changed the spelling of his name for a few years so Americans would pronounce it "cough, not cow") was first sung at St. Bartholomew's at Evensong on January 7, 1906.

FREDERICK SWANN (b. 1931) was a graduate of Northwestern University and Union Theological Seminary's School of Sacred Music. For two years he was concurrently organist-director at the Brick Presbyterian Church and assistant organist at St. Bartholomew's Episcopal Church. In 1957, he was appointed organist and later music director at the Riverside Church. For ten years, Swann was chair of the organ department at the Manhattan School of Music. He moved to California in 1982 as music director-organist at the Crystal Cathedral, Garden Grove (1982–98) and the First Congregational Church, Los Angeles (1998–2001). Frederick Swann was national president of the American Guild of Organists (2002–08) and, since 2001, he has been artist-in-residence at St. Margaret's Episcopal Church in Palm Desert, Calif. and university organist and artist organ teacher at the University of Redlands.

FRANK TAFT (1861–1947) was born in East Bloomfield, N.J., and studied with Clarence Eddy and Samuel P. Warren. He was organist at Clinton Avenue Congregational Church in Brooklyn, and Madison Avenue Reformed Church and Temple Beth-El in New York City. His last church position (until 1912) was as organist of the First Congregational Church, Montclair, New Jersey, where he founded a Bach Choir that gave three-day festivals each year from 1905 to 1910. Taft was a Founder of the

American Guild of Organists, its first auditor, and at one time its national treasurer. In 1901, Taft began his long association with the Aeolian Company as its art director, becoming general manager of the organ department in 1924. He continued with Aeolian-Skinner after the merger of the two companies in 1932, until his retirement in 1942.

F. ANTHONY THURMAN (b. 1966) is a graduate of the University of Louisville and holds a DMA from the Manhattan School of Music. He was director of music at Irvington Presbyterian Church, Irvington-on-Hudson, N.Y, (1994–2016) and is presently director of music of the First Presbyterian Church in Germantown, Pa. He is director of development and communications for the American Guild of Organists.

MAX VOGRICH (1852–1916), was a child prodigy and gave a piano recital at the age of seven. He later went to the Leipzig Conservatory where he studied with Ignaz Moscheles and Carl Reinecke. He toured the world as a pianist and accompanist for August Wilhelmj, and in 1886 settled in New York, left in 1902, but returned at the outbreak of World War I. He was an editor for G. Schirmer, editing the complete piano works of Schumann, among many other works. His 1886 etude, "Staccato Caprice," was long popular with pianists, and his oratorio, *The Captivity,* was given in New York by the Metropolitan Society in 1891.

Since 2011, **JULIAN WACHNER** (b. 1969) has been director of music and the arts at Trinity Church, Wall Street, and in 2018 was named artistic director of the Grand Rapids Bach Festival. He earned a DMA in composition and conducting from Boston University in 1996 and was professor of sacred music at Boston University's School of Theology. He was associate professor at McGill University's Schulich School of Music (2001–11), and director of music of the Church of St. Andrew and St. Paul. Since 2008, he was been conductor of the Washington (D.C.) Chorus. Wachner is an accomplished composer of sacred and secular music, from motets and hymn tunes to opera and symphony.

WAGNER, RICHARD. *See* Norris, Homer.

RODMAN WANAMAKER (1863–1928) was the son of department store magnate John Wanamaker. Upon graduation from Princeton in 1886, he worked in the Philadelphia store, becoming a partner two years later. He was head of the Paris store for ten years, manager of the New York store from 1911, and, on his father's death in 1923, president of the company. He was a pioneer in introducing art and fashion to trade and, to attract customers, held concerts and art and literary exhibitions. He contributed heavily to the development of commercial aviation, owned four Philadelphia newspapers, and subsidized the music programs in both the Philadelphia and New York stores. Both words and music of PEACE were written by Rodman Wanamaker; the hymn was sung before the recessional at his funeral at St. Mark's Church, Philadelphia.

GEORGE WILLIAM WARREN (1828–1902) was born in Albany, N.Y., and though he was graduated from Racine University, he was self-taught in music. He was organist of St. Peter's Church, Albany (1846–58), Holy Trinity, Brooklyn (1860–70), and St. Thomas' Church, Manhattan (1870–1900). The text "God of our fathers, whose almighty hand," was written in 1876 to commemorate the 100th anniversary of the Declaration of Independence. The text was submitted to the 1892 Episcopal hymnal committee and Warren, its editor, composed the tune we know today as NATIONAL HYMN, in celebration of the centennial of the United States Constitution. The text was originally set to Horatio Parker's PRO PATRIA (he was editor of the hymnal), but soon became associated with Warren's thrilling setting.

A native of Montréal, SAMUEL PROWSE WARREN (1841–1915) was organist of New York City's All Souls Unitarian Church (1866–68) and Grace Church (1868–94), except for two years at Holy Trinity Church (1874–76). At Grace Church, he played 230 weekly organ recitals: until then, the most comprehensive series ever given in this country. He was the organ music editor for G. Schirmer where he made masterful transcriptions of orchestral works and edited the first American edition of Mendelssohn's organ works. In 1894, he was forced to resign from Grace Church with the implementation of the then-popular men and boys' choir. The next year he became organist at the First (later Munn Avenue) Presbyterian Church in East Orange, N.J., where he remained until his death. Warren was a Founder of the American Guild of Organists and its honorary president (1902–6). He had a unique career for the last twelve years of his life as an arranger of hundreds of overtures, symphonies, ballets, and piano works that were perforated on Aeolian player organ rolls.

Born in Wales and raised in Denver, DAVID MCK. WILLIAMS (1887–1978) studied in Paris with Vierne, d'Indy, and Widor from 1911 to 1914. On his return to New York, he was appointed organist of the Church of the Holy Communion. After service in the Canadian Artillery (1916–1920), he returned to the church, and six months later, on the death of Arthur Sewell Hyde, was appointed organist and choirmaster of St. Bartholomew's Church. He remained for 27 years until his retirement in 1947.

"Our glowing praise to Thee" was the processional hymn for the annual service of the American Guild of Organists, held at St. Bartholomew's on May 2, 1940. Choirs from four churches joined with that of St. Bartholomew's for a festival EvenSong. Warner Harkins, FAGO, described the service: "In closing, one must pay tribute to the genius and artistry of Dr. Williams. We noted again his fine improvisational flares, sometimes skillfully counterpointed against a unison hymn. Dr. Williams' musicianship is so sensitive and so all-pervasive that any artistic shortcomings in any direction would seem an impossibility."

The text is by Angela Morgan (ca. 1875–1957), a journalist and social advocate, who in 1915, was a delegate to the first International Congress of Women at The Hague. She published several volumes of poems, many of which had appeared in magazines. This poem was one of ten that won a $100 prize in a 1928 competition sponsored by Florence Brooks-Aten for a text for a new national anthem.

RAYMOND HUNTINGTON WOODMAN (1861–1943) was born in Brooklyn and at the age of 19 became organist of the First Presbyterian Church where remained for the next 61 years, one of the longest tenures in the history of American church music. He studied composition and orchestration with Dudley Buck between 1881 and 1885 and, for three months in 1888, studied with César Franck in Paris — the only American to have done so. After 1880, Woodman taught at the Rutgers Institute, the Packer Institute, and was a charter member of the Brooklyn Institute of Arts and Sciences when it was organized in 1891. With G. Donald Harrison, he designed the Institute's (later Brooklyn Museum's) Ernest M. Skinner organ, Opus 758 (dedicated in October 1929), and played monthly Sunday organ recitals from 1930 through 1932. R. Huntington Woodman died after a brief illness on Christmas Day 1943.

ISAAC BAKER WOODBURY (1819–1858) studied music in Boston and when 19 spent a year in London and Paris. He taught for six years in Boston and, in 1849, settled in New York City as director of music at the Rutgers Street Church until ill-health caused him to resign in 1851. He became editor of the *New York Musical Review* and in the fall of 1858 his health broke down from overwork and he went south hoping to regain his strength, but died three days after reaching Columbia, South Carolina. Woodbury is best known for *The Dulcimer; or, The New York Collection of Sacred Music*, one of the best-known hymn collections of the time. He was also one of the compilers of the 1857 *Methodist Hymn Book*.

After studies in Milan, Turin, and the Academy of St. Cecilia in Rome, PIETRO ALESSANDRO YON (1886–1943) came to America and succeeded Gaston Dethier as organist of St. Francis Xavier Church in New York. He remained there until his appointment as music director of St. Patrick's Cathedral in 1928. With the most prominent Catholic church in America as his base of operations, Yon wielded great influence on Catholic church music. His masses and motets were ubiquitous in Catholic churches, as were the Kilgen organs he endorsed and dedicated. His students included Robert Elmore, Norman Dello Joio, and Paul Creston.

JOHN ZUNDEL (1815–1882) was a native of Würtemberg, Germany, who had been encouraged by the organbuilder Eberhard Friedrich Walcker to concentrate on the organ rather than the violin, and was a student of Johann Christian Heinrich. In 1840, Zundel went to St. Petersburg, Russia, to inaugurate the new Walcker organ of St. Paul's and Peter's Lutheran Church — the first documented organ recital given in Russia — and was soon appointed organist of St. Ann's Lutheran Church. He immigrated to New York in 1847 and became organist of Central Methodist Church, Manhattan (1847), St. George's, Stuyvesant Square, (1856), Church of the Saviour, Brooklyn (Feb. 1848–50; 1857), and Plymouth Church (1850–55; 1860–Dec. 1864; Oct. 1866–June 1877). Zundel published several pedagogical texts, a reed organ method, organ music, and edited *The Plymouth Collection* in 1855, with Henry Ward Beecher and his brother Charles Beecher.

The 1875 Geo. Jardine & Son organ in the Brooklyn Tabernacle

INDEX OF COMPOSERS, SOURCES, AND ARRANGERS

INDEX OF FIRST LINES